The Journals
of Brother Roger *of* Taizé

The Journals
of BROTHER ROGER
of TAIZÉ

Volume 3: 1972–1976

CASCADE *Books* • Eugene, Oregon

THE JOURNALS OF BROTHER ROGER OF TAIZÉ
Volume 3: 1972–1976

Cascade Books
An Imprint of Wipf and Stock Publishers
199 W. 8th Ave., Suite 3
Eugene, OR 97401

www.wipfandstock.com

PAPERBACK ISBN: 979-8-3852-1058-9
HARDCOVER ISBN: 979-8-3852-1059-6
EBOOK ISBN: 979-8-3852-1060-2

Cataloguing-in-Publication data:

Names: Brother Roger of Taizé [author].

Title: The journals of Brother Roger of Taizé : volume III: 1972–1976 / Brother Roger of Taizé.

Description: Eugene, OR: Cascade Books, 2024 | Includes bibliographical references and index.

Identifiers: ISBN 979-8-3852-1058-9 (paperback) | ISBN 979-8-3852-1059-6 (hardcover) | ISBN 979-8-3852-1060-2 (ebook)

Subjects: LCSH: Roger, frère, 1915–2005—Diaries. | *Christian Life.* | Spirituality. | Communauté de Taizé.

Classification: BX9459.S38 R64 2024 (paperback) | BX9459.S38 (ebook)

05/10/24

Translation, notes, and commentaries by the Taizé Community.

Contents

Introduction

This book is the third in a series of volumes presenting the journals of Brother Roger, the founder of the Taizé Community in eastern France, an ecumenical community of brothers rooted in the monastic tradition. Today it numbers some eighty brothers, from over twenty-five different countries and from different Christian traditions—Reformed, Lutheran, Anglican, and Catholic—who commit themselves for life to an existence made up of prayer together, work, and hospitality. Each year, tens of thousands of young and not-so-young seekers come to Taizé to spend a week of prayer and reflection in the context of a community life.

Brother Roger was born on May 12, 1915, in French-speaking Switzerland. His father, Charles Schutz, was a pastor in the Swiss Reformed Church, and his mother, Amélie Marsauche, came from a family whose roots were in France. Following his return to the faith after an adolescent religious crisis and a long bout with tuberculosis, he decided to study theology. Convinced that people needed living signs of the gospel to complement the proclamation of the Christian message, he became interested in what today are known as intentional communities.

When the Second World War broke out and the north of France was occupied by the Nazi armies, Roger felt called to leave neutral Switzerland and settle in France. He wanted to be close to the victims of the war, as well as continuing to reflect on the possible creation of a community. In August 1940 he found an abandoned house for sale in the small, isolated hamlet of Taizé, in Burgundy, and purchased it. After the war, Taizé became the home of the community that Brother Roger founded and of which he served as prior until his tragic death on August 16, 2005, at the hand of a demented person, during evening prayer in the church.

Throughout his life, the founder of Taizé was in the habit of jotting down thoughts and reflecting on daily events in notebooks used for that purpose or on small bits of paper. Beginning in 1972, Brother Roger began publishing his diaries. The entries contained in this volume come from two books, *Vivre l'Inespéré* (A Life We Never Dared Hope For), published in 1976 and *Étonnement d'un amour* (The Wonder of a Love), published in 1979.

1972

Brother Roger spent the end of 1972 primarily at Taizé, aside from some short journeys, notably to London, where he met with the archbishop of Canterbury, and to Rome at the end of the year for an audience with Pope Paul VI. But thanks to visits to the hill by friends from places like Brazil, Finland, Africa, as well as contacts by letter and the comings and goings of the brothers, the prior of Taizé remained constantly in touch with the burning questions of church and society.

April 5, 1972

I would go to the ends of the earth if necessary, to the furthest reaches of the globe, to speak over and over again of my confidence in the younger generations, my confidence in the young.

We who are older have to listen, and not condemn. Listen, to grasp the creative intuitions alive within them.

They are blazing trails, they are overturning barriers, they will take the whole People of God along with them. The young will find a way beyond the demarcation-lines which now divide believers from believers; they will invent a reciprocity between believers and non-believers.

As for the elderly, I am convinced that, without them, the world would not be a place worth living in. Those societies, families, or churches that exclude them do not know what they are doing.

Old people who accept their approaching death acquire irreplaceable powers of intuition. They understand with the understanding of the heart. By their loving trust they make it possible for the young, and the not-so-young, to become truly themselves; with their ability to discern the best in others, they release unsuspected sources of life in them.

Every rift between generations works against the sense of the universal.

April 6, 1972

God is so bound up with humankind that wherever there is a human being God is present, whether we like it or not.

April 7, 1972

Two years ago, we chose to begin the preparation of the Council of Youth with an "inner adventure." This meant going against the stream: nowadays people are only too ready to make do with short-lived commitments, with resolves that scarcely last out the week.

Let the living water of Christ come surging up within us, and a whole inner world comes into being, filling the voids. We are borne far beyond all the oppressive ways of life that characterize our civilized societies.

Refuse this freshness offered by the Gospel? Never! However fleeting, it is the happiness of the Beatitudes, the wellspring of poetry, of imagination, and of the ability to kindle flame with the hardest of wood: even broken relationships or the death of someone we love can be used to light glowing fires.

Once launched on this adventure, we realize that it does not stop at ourselves; if it were kept private, it would turn against us. Even at the very beginning, it opens the way irresistibly to encounter with others. It drives us on to a high hill crowned by a "city with her lights shining for all to see."[1]

For two years now, we have set out on an inner adventure. It sustains our vocation to be universal—to be present for everybody.

But who does not dread this inner adventure? It is unsettling. It has the savor of wild fruit, those unexpected finds round a bend in the road. It opens up ways we never dreamed of, paths we had never hoped to find.

April 8, 1972

With one of my brothers, called on Father Buisson.[2] His face shines with peace and mercy. He is already gazing at the invisible. Whoever would have thought it? At age eighty-six, in a way he has replaced John XXIII in my life.

When he was forty, he still could not make up his mind to be ordained, so strong were his scruples, his feelings of guilt and inferiority. "That taught me to understand the people who come to unburden their souls to me."

1. Cf. Matthew 5:14.

2. Parish priest of Culles-les-Roches, a village twenty kilometers from Taizé. See *Brother Roger's Journals*, 2:100.

Still listening, I rise to do what he can no longer do himself: taking three glasses from the cupboard, I pour out the sweet wine and pass round the few biscuits he buys for us when we come.

He asserts that, as far as he can see, his ministry has borne no fruit. When God takes him back to himself, he will know all that his priesthood has achieved.

May 3, 1972

These last three days, the heat has penetrated the farthest corners. Leaning against the edge of the open window, I listen to all the little noises rising from the wood below.

The pansies have faded already, earlier than usual. By the fountain, one or two yellow tulips are still in flower. On both sides of them, cascading down the wall a few yards from my window, are trails of tiny wild flowers, splashes of white and mauve on the other side of the gap which separates us.

May 5, 1972

G. has just arrived from Brazil. He is the only priest for a parish of twenty-eight thousand people near Recife. Infant mortality is high. Children sometimes hold funeral services for other children, among themselves, with no adults present. Sometimes a husband has to bury his wife himself.

May 10, 1972

A South-American Indian leader, visiting us, tells how his brother was killed defending other workers. His attackers clubbed him down viciously, then ran over his body with a truck. His ability to bear his own brother's death and still be eager to help the down-trodden, he attributes to his parents' faith. He asks: how could I truly say I love God if I do not actively love my brothers and sisters? How could I reconcile violent struggle against those who are oppressing my Indian brothers and sisters with the call of the Gospel?

May 20, 1972

Why not receive communion at the Catholic Eucharist? It seems everything is ready for it.

May 21, 1972

Pentecost. Two brothers return from a month spent in Spain. In Galicia and the Asturias they found young people isolated to the point of abandonment—fear strangling their lives. Weep, you who are beloved of God.

Father Arrupe visits us.[3] Not so very long ago, the mere mention of the General of the Jesuits was enough to strike terror into certain hearts. Today, this man is the John XXIII of his order. He is one of the signs of springtime in the church.

May 23, 1972

Tuesday after Pentecost. A road accident a few kilometers away has cost a boy his life.

After the midday prayer, I went to see the driver of the minibus. He was not responsible for the accident; attempting to avoid a motorbike, his vehicle overturned in a ditch. He was sitting in a corner of the church on a low stool. His eyes were bright, clear as deep waters before a storm. Neither of us said a word. I stood there with one hand resting on his bowed head. The other people who had been in the bus when the accident happened gradually

3. Pedro Arrupe (1907–1991), a Spanish Basque priest who served as Superior General of the Society of Jesus from 1965 to 1983. For many years a missionary in Japan, he was in Hiroshima when the atomic bomb fell. He was elected General of the Jesuits at the end of the Second Vatican Council, and worked hard for the renewal of his order in the midst of tensions and incomprehensions from within and without the Society.

gathered round. They had not been told that Hans-Peter had died at the hospital. But as they arrived, our silence made them realize it. I began to pray, with others following in a long, restrained litany.

Later they explained that Hans-Peter, a seventeen-year-old electrical engineer, had only very recently found his way to the faith. The young man driving the bus was the one who had been closest to him during that time.

June 3, 1972

Anniversary of the death of Pope John XXIII. A man capable of looking beyond the immediate situation, he never let himself be upset by warnings that the worst was bound to happen. Three months before he died, two of my brothers and I saw him in tears because his real intentions were being misrepresented. It was the hardest trial of all for him, but he never let himself be caught in that kind of snare. At eighty-two, he surmounted all the obstacles set in his way and succeeded in issuing his last encyclical, *Pacem in terris*. There were any number of attempts to prevent its publication, shortly before his death, but he managed to see it through. In that too he was the universal pastor, taking risks with and ahead of the flock, making no reply to his detractors.

In his old age, John XXIII showed the qualities of a true leader. Others might distort his most disinterested intentions, but he never fell into the pit dug for him. He looked beyond the numerous pressures being brought to bear. If he had based his decisions on reaction to them, he would have been unable to fulfill his charge. If he had begun to justify himself, he would have become bogged down in quicksand. The best way to make the sense of his actions clear was to go still further in the same direction.

June 4, 1972

After today's showers the air is cool, refreshing the very soul. On the hills towards Tournus,[4] the gentle evening light changes from moment to moment. In the valley, cars speeding along—all homeward bound.

June 5, 1972

Evening spent with a young couple active in a labor union. Their struggle is at a low ebb and they feel lost. They find themselves ignored by younger workers who are mainly concerned with improving their financial situation. So we search: what ways are there of overcoming the obstacles? In any passionate search there are times of despondency. There is a future beyond their present situation. And it is clear to them where new birth lies.

June 7, 1972

This Saturday, Hélène and Joseph Barbier, a couple from the village, are celebrating their fiftieth wedding anniversary. We gathered around them today in the village church. They were with us when we first began and they shared in our adventure. For years, it was in their kitchen and downstairs room that our guests had their meals. We have gone through so much together.

June 11, 1972

Just before leaving on a journey, I spend a few minutes with Edith and her husband. It is almost forty years since we last saw one another. She was already engaged when my parents sent me to board at her mother's. She reminds me how, at that time, I spent most of the time talking to her mother, so that she felt rather inferior.

---

4. Tournus, a town twenty-five km east of Taizé, on the Saone River.

Actually I felt intimidated by her seriousness, mistaking it for arrogance!

It was her family, I remind her, that gave me the opportunity of absorbing the Catholic faith. Do you remember, Edith, your mother's devotion to the Eucharist? When she was overwhelmed by difficulties, there she found light.

At the close of the conversation I left to catch the train, and in my heart we went on talking. Do you remember, Edith, the Epiphany celebrations on January 6th, 1929 or 1930? Those festive hours challenged and stirred me. Now Epiphany has become an important celebration at Taizé.

June 21, 1972

This evening there was a television program where young people were given the chance to express themselves freely. That in itself is a breath of fresh air, even though what they have to say is not all of equal value. Why am I so grateful? Because when I was young, I too met with indifference when I tried to raise objections to things which were generally accepted—to the conformist attitude of Christians divided into various denominations, for example. The inertia seemed so great that there were days when I used to tell myself: accept that in your own lifetime you will not see any results from your life's commitment. As a result, today I am so sympathetic towards those who are young. How many of them will succeed in sharing with others the purity of their intentions?

June 29, 1972

Fatima is here, come to see me with other children. For the last few weeks, the face of this little Portuguese girl has worn an expression known only to angels. I begin to tell her a story, making it up as I go along. Her eyes, like two great motionless pearls, listen more than her ears do. She sits bolt upright, quite still. Calm sometimes precedes a storm. Before violent hurricanes nature comes to a standstill, without the slightest breath stirring.

July 3, 1972

In my room, a group from Finland. All Protestants, they have traveled the length and breadth of their country to link up all those preparing the Council of Youth there. The group is led by a married couple. Taisto, the husband, is silent, blond, and energetic, a man of the Far North; he lets his wife, Anna-Maija, do the talking. She is a poet and a writer, brimming over with energy. From time to time he adds something to what she is saying. They point out in an atlas the places where young people meet. There is one on the shores of Lake Inari, north of the Arctic Circle. As their words flow freely, a tinge of the midnight sun shines on our faces. Wild scents, stunted lichens surround us for a fleeting moment.

July 4, 1972

Evening spent with my family. After a period of weakness, my mother is livelier than ever. Paul, her grandson, had brought some flowers he picked this morning two hundred kilometers from here, near the house where she was born. She begins to recall childhood memories she has never spoken of before, and a song she has not sung since her youth. Her face shines with the infinite dignity of long life and poetic joy.

July 5, 1972

All morning long, pouring rain. The waterlogged garden breaks into a symphony of colors. It was not enough for me to see the rain through the windowpanes. As soon as I could spare a moment from work, I ran out to the porch to listen to the drops steadily drumming on the roof. Close by, an umbrella opened and a voice grumbled, "What miserable weather!" Can people be so blind to beauty?

At every stage of life we are granted new harmony. Why dread our failing powers when the years bring inner vision and life gentle as a breath? Could that be the breath of the Holy Spirit? Is that the soul—the secret heartbeat of a bliss beyond words?

A day is rounded when it is like a whole lifetime in miniature. Every moment has its own intensity. Recover the astonishment of each of the fourteen hundred and forty minutes that every day contains. Recover the wonder of these two little pebbles Marc[5] gave me years ago. The smaller is quite flat and dark, with pale streaks. There is a circle at its center.

Every day can bring disappointments, attacks, bitter cups to drink. They are all pitfalls ready to stifle our sense of wonder. Above all, every day offers the expectation of His coming.

A day is round and vast when the worst does not succeed in smothering the Breath of fullness.

July 6, 1972

A girl writes, telling me of her distress after the breakup of her relationship with a boy: "The break is heartrending for me, but I cannot hold it against him. All the other relationships I have, and they are many, are not able to keep me from tasting the full tragedy of human loneliness. I have rarely felt it so strongly. Only Another can give peace."

Her distress has deep roots. It began in the brutality of a father who perhaps never loved her—at least that is what she feels.

---

5. Brother Marc (Heinz Rudolf, 1931–2024), Swiss German brother who worked as an artist in different media. He spent many years with the brothers in Japan and Korea.

July 7, 1972

Today Patriarch Athenagoras[6] enters the life of eternity. With him we lose a man of the same prophetic vein as John XXIII.

He had no lack of trials in his last years. He had realized what changes were necessary in the People of God, but with the situation as it was, he was obliged to suppress the best of his intuitions. Notwithstanding, he was always optimistic. "In the evening, when I retire to my room," he told me once, "I close the door on all my cares and I say: Tomorrow!"

I cannot forget the words he spoke twice to me when I last visited him in Constantinople, two years ago: "I am going to make a confession to you; you are a priest. I could receive the Body and Blood of Christ from your hands." Then the next day: "I could make my confession to you." As we were taking our leave, he added these other words, standing in the doorway and making with his hands the gesture of raising the chalice: "The cup and the breaking of the bread. There is no other solution; remember."

Engraved on my memory, too, is a pilgrimage Max[7] and I made with him around Constantinople during an earlier visit. Every time our car passed a spot where a Christian had died for Christ, he asked the driver to slow down or stop. We made the sign of the cross and then drove on.

July 11, 1972

The newspapers are hopeful that in three weeks' time there will be a peace settlement in Vietnam. The fiery nightmare will be over.

6. Orthodox Patriarch of Constantinople from 1948 to 1972, he worked tirelessly to improve relations with the Catholic and Protestant churches. Brother Roger visited him several times, and a deep understanding grew up between them.

7. Brother Max (Thurian 1921–1996), one of the first four brothers of the community, theologian, with Brother Roger observer at the Second Vatican Council, active in ecumenical movements such as *La groupe de Dombes* and Faith and Order. Ordained a Roman Catholic priest in Naples in 1988 at his own initiative.

If I were ever tempted to forget this drama, the eyes of the young Vietnamese now at Taizé would be enough to remind me. Day after day, those eyes reflect all too well what their people are going through.[8]

July 15, 1972

The essential is always hidden from our eyes. . . . And that lends still more ardor to the quest, and sustains our advance towards the one Reality.

This thought, much in my mind these past few days, could be printed at the front of my next book. . . .

July 19, 1972

The last remnants of the harvest languish under the burning rays of the sun at its zenith. All is ready for the festival of the summer nights. The long phosphorescent dragonflies still hide under the sycamore leaves; soon they will be soaring in their frantic dance.

Now the birds have fallen silent. The only perceptible noise comes from the engines of the mill down by the Grosne, working continuously. The headlights of a lorry there stab through the darkness.

July 21, 1972

Visit of Dom Fragoso. Short and stocky, like the peasants of his region, this bishop has the strength of conviction common to all who live in the Northeast of Brazil.

He does not mince his words. He has radical things to say about European aid to Latin America. No matter how generously intended, it is for him the sign of how dependent the countries of the Southern hemisphere still are. It is too easy for Latin America

8. The Vietnam War had already lasted seventeen years, following quickly in the wake of the Indochinese War waged by the French.

to go on accepting European experts; it would be better to train more of their own people. He sees the same pattern in the church: it is easier for a bishop to call on foreign priests than to train men on the spot. He agrees that certain people, well suited to Latin America, can act as forerunners. But they will have to be ready, like John the Baptist, to step down so that those born locally can grow up.[9]

July 22, 1972

X has been obliged to leave the country he lived in. He bears the marks of that forced departure; his eyes are still full of the horror of the events he witnessed.

"I saw two of my friends," he says, "African priests, led away in handcuffs. When they were about to be shot, they asked for the handcuffs to be taken off so that they could announce the liberation of forgiveness and give absolution to those condemned with them. Then they began to sing, and fell under bullets fired by their own countrymen."

Leaving me, he concludes, "Pray and do something. They are on their own. World opinion knows nothing."

July 23, 1972

This morning, one of the many people waiting to see me is a young mother. With a great deal of difficulty she tells me about the death of her only son, Pierre; he was ten years old. My breath fails as I try to say, "You are still young. I shall go ahead of you into God's

9. During the Second Vatican Council, Brother Roger met Antonio Frago-so (1920–2006), the young auxiliary bishop of Sao Luís de Maranhao, Brazil. He was one of the two bishops who came to Taizé in December 1962, after the first session of the Council, to ask Brother Roger to start a collection to support the farming cooperatives created on church lands in Latin America. That was the beginning of "Operation Hope." Now, ten years later, as bishop of Crateús, the same Dom Fragoso came to say that times had changed and it would be better to stop this aid to Latin America. Just as he listened to him in 1962, Brother Roger followed his advice in 1972.

eternity. There I will speak to Pierre, I promise. Why, even now, Pierre knows that we are here together."

O soul of my soul, weep for the sorrows of all the people I met today! It is He who has to open the way. On the rocky path my step stumbles. . . . But dare to go on, without looking back, head towards wonder, beyond all hope.

What if the ultimate meaning of life were the joy of God in us all?

July 24, 1972

Above my mantelpiece, the icon of the Virgin in the evening shadows. The lamp burning before it reveals the outlines of Virgin and Child.

Since the death of Athenagoras, this icon has gained in importance. I remember how the Patriarch of Constantinople insisted that Max and I choose an icon for Taizé from his cathedral. Embarrassed by the gesture, since we never receive donations or gifts, we accepted the most dilapidated icon we could find, even if that meant restoring it later.

That icon, dimly lit! In the darkness of every Christian's life, a light reveals the outlines of beings and things, and the night glows with a flame that never goes out.

July 31, 1972

Midday meal with young Africans. Improvisation played a trick on us today! Life is made simpler if things are not organized too much ahead of time, but we have to accept the consequences. Certainly the table had been pulled out to its full length, but the sheet used as a tablecloth had not been ironed, and the meal was a frugal one. Paper-thin slices of ham! And there was nothing else left in the kitchen but bread to fill the baskets!

August 2, 1972

Events in China. . . .[10] I have read with enthusiasm so many books and articles about that country over the past twenty years. The brutality of the political upheavals which that nation has undergone across the centuries makes its people all the more appealing. I wonder if the new possibilities of exchange and communication will at last lift the veil which time after time has fallen once again.

August 23, 1972

Laid down my pen to greet a young union organizer from the steel industry. Two words from our conversation stand out: struggle and contemplation.[11] All Christian political involvement is set between those two poles. He speaks with consuming passion of his struggle to free others from every form of oppressive power—not only the power of economic forces, but also at times the power wielded by hidebound labor unions. He is convinced that situations where human beings are most oppressed call forth contemplatives—people capable of living, above all else, the love of Christ.

September 2, 1972

The rays of the setting sun shine golden in one corner of the room, where a vase of autumn flowers has stood since yesterday. As I work, my eyes stray over it constantly.

10. China was still suffering from the turbulent consequences of the cultural revolution launched by Mao Zedong from 1966 to 1969, and the troubles of the following years.

11. The coupling of these two words in this conversation would soon strike Brother Roger as the synthesis of a tension characteristic of the younger generations in those years. He knew that a strong and absolute language was necessary to touch the young, and so those two words together, each one equally demanding, became the central focus of his reflection at Easter 1973 and the title of a book he published in June 1973.

September 5, 1972

Massacre at Munich.[12] A young novice who is passing through remarks: "The Palestinians have really played it well at Munich!" One of my brothers, who is young as well, asks him: Can murder, wherever it comes from, every really win our support? That young novice had given his without hesitating.

September 28, 1972

Visit from Pablo Cano and his wife.[13] Their faces express Andalusia itself! Such eloquent eyes! They have come to ask me if I will say a few words to the family and give a blessing at the wedding of their daughter Adelaida. Where we come from, they say, it is always the head of the family who gives the blessing. Here, our family is you.

September 29, 1972

Went for an hour's outing with a young man from Togo. On the way back, we stop for a moment in the tiny oratory belonging to the sisters in Ameugny.[14] We had only meant to spend a couple of minutes there, but the sisters insist that we come in, and we find ourselves in their living room. The two windows open to the west,

12. During the summer Olympic games in Munich, at a time when the situation in the Middle East was extremely tense, Palestinians belonging to the Black September organization took members of the Israeli delegation hostage and killed two of them. During the assault by the German police, nine other Israeli athletes and five hostage-takers were killed, in addition to a police officer.

13. Pablo Cano belonged to a family from the South of Spain which had been invited by Brother Roger and had been living in the village of Taizé since 1958. See *Brother Roger's Journals*, 2:28, 56.

14. The Sisters of Saint Andrew are an international congregation of women that was founded in Belgium. They follow the spirituality of Ignatius of Loyola, with its accent on availability and discernment. In the 1960s, on a visit to Belgium, Brother Roger invited them to come to Taizé for three months to help with the welcome of visitors. That three-month stay has lasted more than fifty years. They live in Ameugny, the village on the other side of the same hill as Taizé.

towards the setting sun, a glowing ball lighting up ashen clouds. A large Bible is open on the floor.

I suggest that our African guest read aloud a prayer, written by a believer long ago, in the Old Testament:

"Two things I ask, do not refuse them before I die. Take from me falsehood and lying. Give me neither poverty nor wealth. Let me enjoy my share of bread. In abundance, I might betray you and say, there is no God. In deprivation I might steal, and so profane the name of the Lord."[15]

October 7, 1972

Marseilles. Went to pray down in the crypt of St. Victor's church, where Christians have been gathering ever since the third century. Emerging from the crypt, we find a wedding in progress, a young African couple. The bride is covered in veils and lace. The priest invites the sparse congregation to come and give the kiss of peace to the newlyweds. I come forward and say that I will greet them in place of their mothers and fathers. They tell me their names: Marie-Claude and Alex.

October 9, 1972

As the years go by, my brothers' parents become increasingly close and dear to me. Anthony's mother and father are here.[16] I see them walking beneath the trees. At once I leave the young couple I was talking to and run out to them. Spontaneously I embrace them, forgetting that this is an unusual gesture for English people. We make for my room. The conversation is far more than I had imagined. Anthony is their only son, so I would have liked to end by

15. Proverbs 30:7–9.

16. Brother Anthony (Teague, 1942–), from Cornwall, England, spent most of his years in the community as part of a *fraternité* of brothers living in Seoul, South Korea. He taught at the Jesuit university there, translated numerous Korean poets into English, and did extensive research on the origins of Christianity in that country.

telling them that, whatever life may bring, we will always support them. But I could not pronounce the words.

October 25, 1972

Father Buisson[17] has come to us. He is eighty-six and it had been agreed that when he was no longer able to live alone, he would come and live in our house. He is very weak, and spends the day sitting by the fire in our common room. His life has known much inner struggle. It is easy to see in him what makes people of his caliber irreplaceable.

This priest, with all his experience, makes me think of the message Daniel's[18] aged mother wrote for her children before she died: "Do not be sad to see me go, but steep yourselves in thankfulness for all God gives you day after day. Concentrate on what is going well."

November 5, 1972

In Florence with Dom Helder Camara.[19] We have to speak twice, first in a square and then in a stadium during a Mass. I have spent long hours working to be able to say in Italian all that I had prepared.

Any event of this kind is a trial, and at first I had said no. But a chance to say what I think about the way money is used in the church led me to change my mind about my refusal. It is not the speaking that is a trial, but the mass gathering, all the hubbub associated with a large crowd.

17. See entry for April 8, 1972.

18. Daniel de Montmollin (1921–), Swiss, one of the first four brothers. He began the pottery workshop in Taizé and enjoyed international renown as a potter.

19. Helder Camara (1909–1999), archbishop of Olinda and Recife in the Northeast of Brazil, one of the leading figures of the Second Vatican Council, active in the struggle for justice and human rights alongside the poor and a personal friend of Brother Roger's. See *Brother Roger's Journals*, 2:66–67.

Eleven years of friendship with Dom Helder! The better we know each other, the more our meetings are like those of two little children.

My room has a view of the Duomo. I had never seen it by night before, with its subdued lighting. The floodlights caressing its sumptuous architecture surround it with a vast grey hazy cloud, the billowing incense of the three Wise Men.

November 7, 1972

On the way back from Florence, stopped in Romainmotier[20] to listen to the new organ in the church. A warm, fraternal welcome from the pastor, an old friend. A festive meal at his table. He and his wife are attentive to every detail, and this expression of a united couple speaks even more than their words. The church's stonework shimmers in hazy sunlight. Music makes the fullness which is in God more accessible—as though the heavens were rent and a few notes from the invisible slipped through.

November 11, 1972

Dancing light sparkles on the nasturtiums hanging down over the trough. Warmth in the mid-November air. People say, "The seasons are not what they used to be." Certainly, with the roses still blooming, you begin to wonder.

November 20, 1972

Return after two days in London. A meeting in a poor part of town with young people from every region of England, with a few of their pastors. The meeting ended with a public service in St. Paul's Cathedral. It was quite something, in that venerable church, to see

20. Romainmotier, location of a former priory founded by the monks of Cluny in the canton of Vaud, Switzerland.

the young people sitting on the floor on their coats and blankets, celebrating the resurrection with a little candle in their hands!

A conversation with the archbishop of Canterbury.[21] He is a man close to the sources. Many young people are looking forward to his visit to Taizé next year. We expect prophetic words from him.

December 1, 1972

Departure for Rome. December is already here, but the morning sunlight is so strong that the lime trees cast deep shadows across the still-green grass. The last roses are gleaming. To be forced to leave these skies. . . .

December 2, 1972

First evening in Rome. Went for a walk as far as the Piazza Navona, lined with stalls. One has rag dolls for sale; I choose one with a red blouse, a flat laughing face and long dangling legs, to take home as a present for one of the children. The young stall-keeper is surprised: we met at Taizé last summer.

December 9, 1972

Last night at eight, conversation with the pope. Paul VI had carefully read the report in which I had tried to analyze certain characteristic trends of present-day consciousness. My question was: how to face up to these trends and not reject them? Or, in the language of the Gospel, how not to abolish but to fulfill?[22]

---

21. Michael Ramsey (1904–1988), archbishop of Canterbury from 1961 to 1974. A respected theologian, he worked for closer relations with the Orthodox and Catholic churches.

22. See Matthew 5:17.

After our conversation, we went to the chapel for a simple prayer and a moment of silence. "I know how fond of silence you are at Taizé," the pope says.

Then we continue our conversation at table, over a meal. My heart is full on finding the pope so able to understand the way young people think. As we part, he insists, "If you have the key for understanding the young, tell me what it is."

I would like to have such a key, but I know that I do not have it, and never shall.

1973

The diary entries depict 1973 as a fairly quiet year. A note of serenity is perceptible in the reflections, which does not negate the underlying difficulties and struggles. Preparations for the Council of Youth go forward, and Brother Roger is affected by the premature death of Brother Christophe at age fifty from a brain tumor, and the passing of his mother at the end of the year.

January 24, 1973

The day is dying on the bare earth in the garden below. Six in the evening. In a few minutes, the owl will begin to call its mate with long, repeated cries. Gregoire[1] drops in for a moment; we speak a few words and night has fallen. Yan's[2] two windows shine like two pale eyes.

January 28, 1973

Paris. Night of prayer in the church of St. Ignace. Those who like improvisation must have been delighted. At the start, the church was so packed that the young people still in the street outside had to be invited to come back later, when others had left.

This morning, the skies of Paris reflected our joy at being alive. Four of us crossed the Seine by the Pont des Arts, then went into the Tuileries Gardens. Distant perspectives opened around the Arc de Triomphe and the high-rise buildings of the Defense. That was our morning's goal: foreground blending into background, harmonious progressions added century after century by human hands.

February 21, 1973

One of the brothers receives a phone call from the mayor of a near-by village. Recently a childless widow died there, and on opening her will the lawyer discovered that she had left her house and estate to our community. We wrote quickly to say that we refused this bequest, in the same way as the community has always refused to accept gifts.

1. Brother Grégoire (Gérard Huni, 1933–1997), from a French and Swiss family. He spent many years in Africa, in the *fraternités* of brothers in Algeria, Rwanda, Kenya, and Senegal.

2. Brother Yan (Johannes Fentener van Vlissingen, 1929–1995), a psychologist from the Netherlands who wrote among other things on celibacy in the religious life.

February 27, 1973

At his weekly audience last Wednesday, Pope Paul referred to our life here. Talking about the young, he stressed how many of the young people at Taizé seek silence.

March 2, 1973

In the mail, a letter from a woman who writes to thank me for *Ta fête soit sans fin*. The mother of three young children, she is seriously ill. She reads to calm her anguish after her family has left her at the end of visiting time. She concludes: "Today my children arrived and said: here is a bit of spring for you. The smallest of the girls was hidden behind a whole branch of forsythia. So I am sending you a twig of it in advance for your birthday, because by that time I shall no doubt be myself in the festival that has no end."

March 4, 1973

In church this morning, after I had spoken with a number of people, a little girl came up and asked, "Could you teach me how to confess?" There was a burden weighing on her frail shoulders. How can an eight-year-old child be so imprisoned in guilt? "Who can condemn us, since Jesus is praying for us."[3] I would like to make my Easter morning sermon a meditation on those words.[4]

March 7, 1973

Discussed the meaning of Lent with a young pastor, who is spending a few days in retreat here. Lent: forty days granted us in which to marvel at a love too great for words.

3. Brother Roger is quoting from a hymn often sung at Taizé; the words are taken from Romans 8:34.
4. See page 117.

April 6, 1973

Today, can there be any other road for Christians than the one with a name which is hard to write—the way of holiness? I am reluctant to call the young to follow it. Too many of their elders might well smother so dazzling a flame.

April 17, 1973

Conversation with two young men, standing beside the icon of the Virgin in the church. They have been preparing to become priests, but hesitate to take the final step. Every human being is full of inner contradictions, the present is a time of enormous changes, and the value of the ministry is frequently disputed: all of which makes them realize that being a "witness" today means being a "martyr," the original meaning of the word.

April 18, 1973

Wide awake at five this morning, I go down into the woods. From the back of her kennel, the dog sees me go by. I make signs so that, although she licks my hands as usual, she will not wake up the whole house by yelping. She understands my language. If only we too could understand the language of the birds flying away beneath the branches, disturbed in their morning chorus!

April 23, 1973

Easter Monday. It was no mean feat, for all who had worked to prepare these last days' meeting, to welcome such a mass of people.

Reflected on the way we go forward together. Since the announcement of the Council of Youth, part of my responsibility has been to listen and sum up with others—not only with the intercontinental teams, but also spontaneously with one or another. In exceptional circumstances my service could also be to arbitrate, but that has never been necessary. We have never been brought to a standstill. That only goes to show how great is the vitality inspiring each and every one; during the last three years, the path has sometimes been steep.

May 6, 1973

The situation in the Middle East is getting worse. There is talk of a black May, after a black September. Some of the *fedayin*,[5] condemned more and more by public opinion, are growing increasingly desperate. What can we do for people who are slaughtering one another? This morning, during my weekly meeting with the young people, I dwelt on this topic. Afterwards, I discovered that there was an Arab Christian from Amman present, on his way back home. He came to talk with me.

May 17, 1973

A dream: we are approaching a harbor but, as we are about to land, we find ourselves being driven back out to sea.

May 18, 1973

Week made heavy by a brother's illness. Christophe[6] is at death's door. The doctors have discovered a brain tumor. At the hospital, between two periods of coma, I was able to tell him, "Your mother is praying with you." She died many years ago, but we often used to speak about her.

5. The fedayin were Palestinian fighters. In September 1970, in retaliation for an attack against the king of Jordan, an action by the Jordanian army led to the death of thousands of Palestinians.

6. Brother Christophe (Walter von Wachter, 1923–1973), from Germany, was a prisoner of war in Russia after the Second World War. He insisted that the community make visits to Christians in Eastern European countries during the Cold War. As a brother he worked for many years at the World Council of Churches.

May 29, 1973

A German girl, on the point of leaving, remarks, "When we return home, we shall be back in the world, while you all stay here." But everyone takes "the world" with them, wherever they are. It is with them in teeming crowds as well as in solitude, and even in dreams, when we consider ourselves far removed from everything by sleep.

June 9, 1973

To get from others what we want, in Christian circles—and elsewhere too—how often we either play upon people's guilty consciences, or else make prophecies of doom.

June 12, 1973

A letter from Jacques.[7] He is in India. He speaks about the encounter with Hinduism and Buddhism. They oblige us to leave our familiar world completely, whereas here in the West even Marxism and humanism, with which we try to dialogue, are still secularized derivatives of Christianity.

June 17, 1973

Trinity Sunday. This morning Christophe died. I want to join my brothers, who are also suffering from this loss, but an hour alone is a comfort. Until the very end, I had hoped that he would be spared, even if as an invalid. In recent months, well before his accident, I had imagined him living among us as a *starets*.

---

7. Brother Jacques (Schiesser, 1940–2019), Swiss theologian. He spent many years in the community's *fraternités*, first in the United States (Madison, Chicago . . .) then in Bangladesh, where he taught for many years at the Catholic seminary in Dhaka.

June 20, 1973

Listen, listen, never force things. My responsibility imposes a certain solitude, and I want to consent to it. If I could be aware every day that this portion of solitude is reserved solely for Him. . . . Listen, never force things. Understand with the heart, the mind will catch up later.

July 10, 1973

Once again, during a private conversation, I hear a familiar question: How can I be myself? How can I fulfill myself? These questions preoccupy some people to the point of anguish.

I remember what Johan[8] once said, talking of his encounter with Jesus: "He does not say, be yourself; he says, be with me." How right he is! Christ does not tell us "Find yourself" or "Run after yourself." He says, "You, follow me!"

If "being oneself" means dropping our masks, giving up conformist attitudes and conventions, who would disagree? That is not just good; it is vital.

On the other hand, a person is chasing illusions if, in the quest to be themselves, their ego so asserts itself that it exists at the expense of other people's freedom, and swells up like a leech.

A person growing like this on the backs of others, at their expense, may not necessarily exclude God from their life. But although God is not rejected, he is far from being what really matters.

When the Gospel asks people to be themselves and to develop their gifts and talents a hundredfold, it is not in order to serve their own ends; it is to serve others.

In the Gospel, to be oneself means searching deeply until the irreplaceable gift given to each one of us is discovered. Through that special gift, unlike anyone else's, each person is brought to fulfillment in God.

So keep silence, withdraw into the desert, if only once in a lifetime, and discover that gift. . . .

8. Brother Johan (Danell, 1944–), from Sweden.

July 11, 1973

With so many people giving up the faith, there are Christians who console themselves with the thought that there will always be a "small remnant." But what then becomes of the vocation to be universal, to be a leaven of communion in the midst of humanity? Joy at being part of the "small remnant" of the People of God can easily turn into the self-satisfaction of exclusive minorities.

July 16, 1973

Yesterday evening, paused for a long time beside the oak tree at the bend in the path, looking at the sky. At ground level, the branches were rustling in a faint breeze. High above, the clouds were dancing in the light of the full moon, driven by squall after squall from west to east.

Back in my room again, sitting perched on the windowsill with my feet dangling above the porch roof, I could not tear my eyes away from the windblown clouds. The moon appeared and disappeared. Whenever it was veiled, the night became incandescent.

During prayer this morning, the conviction came that no burden would be too great. Everything seemed desirable. And now the day continues, bathed in that peaceful light, with the certainty of a presence.

Why are such moments of intensity so easily forgotten, as though they had never been? It is not a waste of time to note them down.

August 4, 1973

Long talk with Ivan Restrepo. He has just spent five years writing a doctoral thesis on Taizé. Only a Jesuit, and a South American one at that, would ever have had the courage to spend so long on such a task. I really cannot understand why Taizé is chosen as a thesis topic in universities. How many students have we already dissuaded? To understand the life we are trying to live, the necessary perspective is not yet there, even for ourselves. As for Ivan, those who have read his thesis say it is of real value.[9]

August 8, 1973

There are people who always want to be in at the start. If they have not been involved in the initial stages of a creation, they do not care to be associated with it. Do they not realize that there is no more creativity present at the beginning of a venture than later on? Creativity is sometimes expressed more in continuity and duration. Otherwise all that remains is the short-lived adventure. And when the dazzling fireworks have burned out, we are left in the dark.

For us here at Taizé, creativity is just as manifest in the last twelve years as it was in the first ones.

September 4, 1973

Relived intensely an evening in the summer of 1942, when I was still on my own at Taizé. I was sitting writing at a small table. I knew that I was in danger because of the political refugees I was sheltering in the house. The risk that I would be arrested was considerable. Members of the civilian police force had repeatedly made raids and questioned me. That evening, with fear in the pit of my stomach, a prayer took hold of me. I said it to God without really understanding what I was saying: "Take my life if you think fit, but let what has begun here continue." Yet what had been begun in those two years? Principally a welcoming house and prayer in solitude.

9. The thesis of this Colombian Jesuit, defended at the Gregorian University in Rome, was published in Spain in 1975: Ivan Restrepo, *Taizé, una busqueda de comunión con Dios y con los hombres*, Ediciones Siguemi, Salamanca.

September 5, 1973

Long talk with a small group of young men and women. They take a large share in the responsibility for making people welcome here. We discuss the Council of Youth, now in preparation.

In the Northern hemisphere at present we are confronted with a breakdown of "moral memory."[10] One expression of this is the rejection of faithfulness in all its forms. Everything has to be lived in the present moment.

This loss of "moral memory" was becoming a vital question for our ecumenical vocation in Taizé, and then an answer appeared: to prepare a Council of Youth. The very idea of taking four and a half years together in order to prepare ourselves for something which itself will last for years is in itself a challenge.

The Council of Youth will be no ordinary adventure. It will not be a congress or a forum, a platform for ideas in vogue. To have chosen to call it a Council means that it is an adventure lived in the Body of Christ, his church—that irreplaceable communion set in the midst of a suffering, searching world, a world that, without realizing it, aspires after a new birth.

September 16, 1973

Some people jealously treasure in their hearts a piece of broken glass. It scratches them whenever they like and with it they are apt to scratch those around them.

September 20, 1973

Those children who often come and kneel beside me in church during the common prayer. . . . What they discover will mark them for life. So never deprive a child of that current of contemplation which will carry them onward their whole life long.

---

10. The expression is from Dietrich Bonhoeffer in his *Letters and Papers from Prison.*

September 21, 1973

Here again, at the round table with its timeworn pinewood top. The very sight of the wood awakens dreams of childhood in the Jura Mountains. In every poor villager's home, the pinewood surfaces shone brightly, polished with much rubbing of cloths.

An hour as well-rounded as the table, everything coming together. No discontinuity between the hours of my youth and those of today. They nourish one another,

Sitting on the little stool, also of pinewood, I take up my pen once again, like a craftsman irresistibly called to labor on and on.

September 25, 1973

Conversation with a scientist. A high price must be paid for great gifts of intelligence, or for genius. The other sides have to be accepted as well, and they are on a par with the abilities.

October 1, 1973

Visit from the archbishop of Canterbury.[11] Speaking to the young people here, he says, "The Council of Youth will not be one more organization, or a new movement. By means of it many young people will help the church, all over the world, to become a church able to forget itself, laying aside all pride, all power, all wealth."

October 15, 1973

In the preparation of the Council of Youth, some of the tensions that arise come from persons rather than ideas. Far from bringing us to a standstill, they help us to go forward. What will matter in the end will be the communion continually rediscovered. All the rest will pass, without leaving much of a trace.

11. See note for November 20, 1972.

As for our community, its vocation to live an anticipation of communion in the church is even more precise than we had imagined. We are asked to keep on striving after a certain sense of perspective and inner silence, and to go on taking risks.

October 23, 1973

For a brother's birthday meal, we invited Cristobal. We talk about the flooding in southern Spain. He recalls how, when he was ten, in Malaga he saw a river burst its banks and a torrent of water and mud come crashing down. Before his very eyes, the house of his best friend, Eduardo, was destroyed. As the walls collapsed he saw Eduardo's body being swept away by the waters. During the whole of the next week, every day he spent time in the local church, before the reserved Sacrament. He wrestled with God, asking why Eduardo was gone. After eight days he found peace. He had told God, "You are all I have." At that point in his story, Cristobal began to cry; he wept for a long, long time. We decided to leave the dessert for another time and Cristobal promised, "I will come and sing flamencos." At table tonight, tirelessly, Cristobal sang.

October 24, 1973

Gather everything that happens, trivialities included, without reservation, regret, or nostalgia, in inexhaustible wonder.

Set out and move forward, one step at a time, from doubt towards faith, not worrying about the impossible that lies ahead. Light a fire, even with the thorns that tear you.

October 26, 1973

Situations sometimes arise in which a young couple can see no other way of maintaining their unity than by making a clean break with father and mother. But a break of that kind brings only temporary peace, since for basic stability it is so essential to have father and mother integrated in oneself.

Never allow oneself to be guilt-ridden because of the frustration of a father who, without realizing it, had a passion for his daughter, or a mother overattached to her son. Those parental attitudes are as old as the hills. Parents often have no control over their possessive love, the result of inner distress. It is important to understand them as best one can, and above all not to imprison them by our condemnation.

November 17, 1973

In Paris to see Cardinal Silva of Santiago in Chile, who is on a brief visit to France.[12] It took me a few seconds to recognize him; his face had grown gaunt and deeply furrowed. But the eyes remained unchanged.

It is obvious that people are suffering in other countries too. But the tragedy of Chile brands many with a hot iron, leaving them completely at a loss. It must be said that one day we were given the possibility of intervening from Taizé to save a human life, that of Luis Corvalan, the General Secretary of the Chilean Communist Party. . . . In that precise instance, I received clear proof of the courage of Pope Paul VI.[13]

November 18, 1973

During a meeting, Cristobal told all the young people here: "We have to pass through the Garden of Olives,[14] to know what it means to be abandoned by others, seemingly even by God, so as to reach the point where we can abandon ourselves in God. I am drawing

---

12. Raúl Cardinal Silva Henriquez (1907–1999), archbishop of Santiago de Chile from 1961 to 1983, an outspoken opponent of the military regime of Augusto Pinochet.

13. See entry for January 6, 1975.

14. See Luke 22:39–46.

near to that garden, I am still at the gate, not daring to enter but knowing that I must, if I want to accompany Christ, to wait with him for Easter to come, and pass on to new life."

December 2, 1973

Yesterday, in the waiting room at Macon railway station, we encounter three immigrant workers from Algeria. We begin to talk. Two of them have small children. Once a year they go to spend a few weeks with their families in North Africa. They make no embittered remarks as they tell of their difficulties at work, or when they look for lodgings. We are indebted to them for part of the development of Europe, and for the rise in our standard of living. Yet very many Europeans continue to treat them as outcasts.

December 4, 1973

For the last few days nothing more could be done for my mother; she could no longer take nourishment. This morning she was eager to reassure everyone, and to Ghislain[15] she said, "Life is beautiful," adding, "We should always be joyful." This afternoon she murmured once more, "Life is beautiful," then repeated several times, "*Jésus . . . c'est beau*." Those were her last words. At eight this evening, while we were in church praying, she entered Christ's eternity. She passed away gently, her breath simply slowing to a halt.

A few years ago, after her first heart attack, as soon as she could speak again she uttered these words, "I am not afraid to die, I know in whom I believe, . . . but I love life."

December 15, 1973

Paris. During Mass at St. Sulpice, the priest preaches on the meaning of community. In every community, there must be one person

---

15. Brother Ghislain (Jean-Paul Mazure, 1942–), a medical doctor from Belgium, was the first Catholic brother to enter the community.

who sees that the whole body does not settle down in self-satisfaction, but opens more and more towards the universal.

So when you are ashamed of not being capable of fulfilling your role, when you sometimes long to tear off the copper cross you wear over your prayer robe, remember that moment: "In every community, there must be one person. . . ."

December 16, 1973

No fears for the salvation of humanity. God is love. For those who know this, fullness lies there. And as for those who have never known anything of God, it was to visit them that Jesus went down "to the lower regions" on Holy Saturday.[16] He went down to every human being who had died before him. And now, every moment, he continues to visit those who do not know him. . . .

16. See Ephesians 4:9.

1974

1974 was above all the year of the opening of the Council of Youth, which had been prepared since Easter 1970. From August 30th to September 1st, many thousands of young adults from throughout Europe and from other continents made their way to an out-of-the-way village in Burgundy; it was by far the largest gathering ever held on the hill of Taizé. In his journal, Brother Roger was more concerned with the meaning of the event and how it would be lived out by the participants when they went back to their everyday lives. This was also a year of visits to the United States, to London to receive the Templeton Prize, to Austria and Germany, to Rome, and, at year's end, to Latin America.

January 1, 1974

What if this year, 1974, were to be the year for us to abandon everything in God; the burden is so excessive and the means so limited. What if this year we were to let the Holy Spirit turn us into people of overflowing fullness? Without an overflowing heart, without a grasp of situations, everything shrinks; our vision of people and events becomes increasingly narrow.

January 3, 1974

Letter from a student: "I left for Taizé on my own, hesitant about taking a step that would commit me further in the steps of Christ. Now I see, or more precisely I sense, how far I have come in nine days spent on the hill. I have expressed my attachment to Jesus Christ struggling to save all people. In the fatigue of a sleepless night I lived with Jesus Christ struggling in the Garden.[1] During the community prayer every day, sitting on my heels, as I looked at you brothers I thought, God really does call us to madness, to live a life both so far from and so close to the world.

"I am studying economics. For the last eighteen months I have been faced with concrete problems of violence, psychological because of the absurdity of the subject-matter, physical as regards the police or extremist right-wing groups, or even the apathy of the great mass of students. Last summer I opted to become a militant for revolution, and the more I struggle, the more festival quickens me.

"If tomorrow I have to give my life, I know that, somewhere, others have done so before me."

January 11, 1974

For my brothers gathered in the little village church, I comment on a story in the Old Testament.

---

1. See Luke 22:39–46.

One day in the village called Zarephath,[2] at a time of serious famine, an old woman sees Elijah, the man of God, come into her house. There is very little left in her oil-jar and her flour-bin. But she does not hesitate to use it all to make three cakes, saying: "Afterwards, we shall have nothing but death to look forward to."

She pushes her trust to its utmost limits. At that point, God passes by like a flash of light. The flour and oil are never going to give out.

This year, with the opening of the Council of Youth approaching, there is not much flour in our sacks, and very little oil in our jars. But with this little, overabundance is offered, unfailingly.

Committed to venture into the unknown for Christ, we can already tell him: I have taken you at your word; I regret nothing. If I had to begin all over again, I would take the same road.

January 15, 1974

Today, as in the past, our community is continually roused to new efforts by the "church's torment," as one of my brothers put it.

We are called to be part of a double movement: on the one hand to renew from within, untiringly, all that can be renewed in the People of God; and on the other hand, to dare to place ourselves in the front lines.

Over the last ten years there has been much reawakening in the People of God throughout the world. Everywhere conformist habits are changing into personal adherence.

The march of this people is slow, but none the less sure. Any attempt to hasten it is sure to arouse panic.

It involves making the values of popular belief our own and giving them new life from within, entering into the heart of the masses so as to share their aspirations, hopes, and distress.

Passion for communion in the Body of Christ, his church, entitles no one to ride roughshod over the People of God in its slow progress. Anyone who would plunge the great mass of Christians

2. 1 Kings 17:8–24.

into hopelessness in that way would be heartless. Very often it is childlike faith which has been passed on to them. Is anybody entitled to tie a stone around the neck[3] of the simplest member of God's People and so wound the Body of Christ himself?

There are those sturdy enough to stand at the forefront of the church's life; they take the risks and prepare the ways forward. Already, all over the world Christians are becoming brothers and sisters of non-believers; that is one of the clear signs of our time. Christians everywhere are becoming more and more aware that they are part of the whole human community and are called to be leaven of unity in a secularized world.

Keep within the body of the whole People of God, stay in the church's front lines: there is no contradiction in those two aims.

Until my last breath, I will use all the strength of my conviction to urge the greatest possible number of people to follow that way.

February 6, 1974

In the United States with Robert[4] and Thomas.[5] Delight at discovering San Francisco. This is the second invitation from the bishops of the Anglican communion, this time to speak about the Holy Spirit.[6]

At present, when there is a revival of the Spirit, how can gifts and charisms be lived in a way that complements, and not excludes, one another?

Among all the young people I listen to at Taizé, those known as charismatics are often a real refreshment. But I feel obliged to say: if I try to understand what the Spirit is saying to the church

---

3. See Matthew 18:6.

4. Brother Robert (Giscard, 1922–1993), the fifth brother to enter the community and the first Frenchman. A medical doctor, he was also an avid musician and, with the composer and organist Jacques Berthier, created the short musical phrases known throughout the world as the songs of Taizé.

5. Brother Thomas (Ian Williamson, 1939–2019), from Scotland.

6. See *Brother Roger's Journals*, 2:103–4.

through you, try in your turn to discover what the Spirit is saying through those who have other points of view—an unselfish political struggle, for example. Listen and understand.

At the same time I tell others: the charismatics experience a release in their very depths, a heightened sensitivity, allowing them to express freely a whole range of human possibilities that have hitherto remained latent.

March 2, 1974

After the lowering skies of late February, and then yesterday's squalls, today the wind has thinned the clouds, here and there piercing openings in the dark masses. All morning long a *tachiste* painting kept appearing and then melting away. Look with new eyes, and learn to love even the subtle lighting of these days.

March 3, 1974

Ivan Restrepo writes to announce the death of Diego, one of his young Jesuit brothers. I knew him. When he was studying in Lyons, before he returned to Colombia, he used to come to Taizé. He died of cancer, in the space of a few weeks. Living in an iron lung, he could only communicate by writing notes. On the morning of February 13 he wrote, "Is it serious?" Ivan, who was near him, did not hide the truth. At the end of the morning he wrote, "Roger's book." They brought it. A few minutes later he wrote, "If I die, put these words on my grave: may your festival never end."[7] He fell asleep, and died soon after.

Diego's last wish will bear me along until my race reaches its goal.

7. A reference to the French title of Brother Roger's book of 1971, *Ta fête soit sans fin.*

March 4, 1974

Letter from a Catholic bishop who recently spent a few days with us: "In Taizé, everything is already full of high expectancy for the Council of Youth. You feel yourself caught up by a rushing wind of the Spirit that is shaking the church to its very foundations, not trying to destroy, but eager to break down walls in order to prepare it to welcome great multitudes searching for a hope capable of giving life to the world, and of inspiring the younger generations to build a world of justice and fraternity, signs of the Kingdom to come. It is only natural that this expectancy is mingled with anxiety; it involves abandoning oneself to the Spirit, with whom there is no telling where things will end; all human reckoning is upset. I have a strong feeling that the Council of Youth, in spite of all the trials, the resistances, the inevitable gaps and failures, will be a new step forward for the church and for all humankind. To staid, realistic Christians that hope may seem ridiculous and excessive, but the parable of the mustard seed,[8] and the parable of the little carpenter who becomes the risen Lord, is a utopia that never fails to come into being despite all predictions to the contrary. Pentecost is not over yet."

March 13, 1974

Thought several times recently of what should have been my first book. I am sorry now that I destroyed the manuscript, as I destroy all my old papers. That manuscript would have told me something about the choices I made when I was young.

If I had published *Evolution of a Puritan Boyhood* at the time I wrote it, when I was twenty, my life would probably have taken another turn. Why was I unable to rewrite the end of the book the way Jean Paulhan, director of the *Nouvelle Revue Française*, suggested? He would have published it if I had. Why was I so convinced that my manuscript formed a whole as it stood, and

8. Matthew 13:31–32.

therefore could not be modified? It was the outcome of the combat and discoveries of my early youth.

March 25, 1974

A priest who tries to be priest and layman at the same time denies the laity its own specific ministry—he wants to be everything at once.

March 29, 1974

Two young refugees from Chile, recently in Taizé, said, "Here you are called to sow and sow again, without worrying about the harvest."

April 5, 1974

Over the last few years, have spoken to so many young men who have given up the idea of becoming priests. They are afraid of finding no community, and so of being plunged into a solitude more exposed than ever before. I ask myself whether the time has not come to ordain married men?

For over a thousand years, in the Catholic church celibacy and priesthood have gone hand in hand, and I know what this centuries-old tradition signifies. Still, the sharp drop in priestly and pastoral vocations poses a question.

The present upheavals in the church have their roots in the enormous transformations that our human societies are undergoing. It is not true that God is punishing his church; he is carrying her forward more visibly than ever before. He is not creating a vacuum. Already, at the same time as the life-blood of vocations is being lost, he offers a means of healing—the ministry in which every baptized member of the laity shares is being developed in new, unforeseen ways.

Certainly, local communities animated by courageous lay people will go far. But can they do without somebody to bring them all together and to preside at the Eucharist, the source and fulfillment of all communion? Surely, when married men demonstrate the obvious ability to become such gatherers and animators, does not a question arise demanding an answer? Can we go on depriving local communities of such shepherds?

Admittedly, the experience of some Protestant pastors' families can make us wonder. There are children who lived trapped in "minister's family" situations. But on the other hand, there are all those wives devotedly assisting their husbands in their ministry, not to mention the host of children of Orthodox priests and Protestant pastors, active in the workaday world, who ensure the living continuities of Christ, because their childhood was nourished by the essence of their father's ministry.

Has the time come for the Catholic church to confer the priesthood on married men? I raise the question with the authority given by the fact that I came to Taizé and called others to choose to live a whole lifetime committed to celibacy in community. That has shown me the quality of mystical communion that celibacy brings. If we made all the commitments to life in community, except for celibacy, we would never realize how utterly men can be consumed with passion for communion in the Body of Christ.

April 6, 1974

Anyone who lives for themselves alone is more dead than alive. If the aim of living is merely to last as long as possible, existence has no meaning. All who consent to lose their life hear a call beyond themselves.

April 8, 1974

Tomorrow in London. This is only the second time the Templeton Prize is being awarded.[9] When I learned that I had been chosen, I thought of Mother Teresa receiving it last year, and of my brothers working with her among the dying in Calcutta.

Accept this award for reconciliation in simplicity of heart, solely as a confirmation offered by other believers—Buddhists, Hindus, Muslims, Jews, and Christians—to the believer you try to be, day after day.

The large sum of money attached to the award will not be for the community. We have always refused gifts, living by our work alone, without any capital reserves. Neither can I accept it to offer hospitality to people coming to Taizé, even though our funds have given out for the time being.

I and others asked the young people staying on the hill in recent weeks to whom the money should go. It will be given to young people, particularly in the Southern hemisphere, who are committed to paths of struggle and contemplation, striving to be untiring seekers of communion. Part of it will go to young people in the British Isles who are working to provide a welcome to immigrants from Africa and Asia, and to others striving for reconciliation in Northern Ireland.

April 10, 1974

More often than ever before, people ask me, "What is the most important thing in your life?"

Unhesitatingly I reply: our community prayer and, in it, the periods of silence.

Then, immediately after that, the best thing in my life: when I am talking with someone alone, to perceive their whole being,

---

9. The "Templeton Prize for Progress in Religion" was founded by the philanthropist Sir John Templeton in 1972. At first awarded to spiritual leaders of different traditions, it gradually focused more on the intersection of science and religion.

the critical experiences they can scarcely bear to reveal, the knot of a permanent failure or discord in the inner life, but also the unique gifts through which the life of God in them is able to bring everything to fulfillment.

Far from being disconcerted when they reveal to me what they can hardly bear to put into words, I try to comprehend them as a whole person, by means of a few words or attitudes rather than by lengthy attempts at explanation.

Intuition comes to the aid of understanding, most fully itself when called upon to grasp all that the other person is going through. Sensitivity, sharpened with the years, has a part to play as well. Nowadays my time is far more limited than it used to be, so I am all the more alert to grasp instantly what really is at stake.

It is not enough to share those hidden things that have caused a person's wounds. It is even more vital to search for that special gift of God, the pivot of their whole existence. Once this gift—or gifts—has been brought to light, all roads are open.

No dwelling on the knots, tragedies, failures, and conflicting forces; hundreds of contradictory reasons for them can always be found. Move on as quickly as possible to the essential: uncovering the unique gift, the talents entrusted to every human being, which are meant not to lie buried but brought to full life in God.

The best thing in my life? I could go on for ever: those rare occasions when I suddenly find myself free to drop everything and go out . . . walking for hours and conversing in the streets of some great city . . . sharing a meal with guests around a table . . . the sight of a brother coming into my room, and admiring in his transparency, his honesty with himself, his refusal to be drawn into labyrinths. . . .

April 11, 1974

What will today bring for the young man who waited yesterday in the church until everyone else had gone, so as to be the last to speak to me? A little way off, his wife was looking on. Through what he said, I sensed the long-standing split within him which today leads him to one breakup after another. What will his future be? I am confident. What he had always kept bottled up has somehow exploded; he was able to express it at last. Slowly everything will fall into place. I expect a letter from him.

What will today bring for F.? I discovered him yesterday too. He is about to leave for Mexico, as a political exile. "Do your parents know what is happening?" I asked. "No, they are simple people; they could never understand. It would kill my mother." He does not complain. He simply came to greet me and to receive the blessing of Christ. He explains that this moment will take the place of saying farewell to his elderly parents.

April 16, 1974

Easter Week. One thing that can already be clearly sensed about the Council of Youth is that it will not be able to make do with people who only commit themselves halfway; it can only use young men and women who, step by step, commit themselves totally.

We will never proselytize, neither for the Council of Youth itself, nor for anybody in the world. We are not setting ourselves free from cold, authoritarian, doctrinaire systems only to rush headlong into other systems which are bound to imprison, however tempting they may appear.

April 18, 1974

So many people hide behind their own words! It sometimes happens that those who are least committed to Christ and to justice succeed in disguising their lack of commitment by professing with their lips irrefutable ideals or doctrines.

April 26, 1974

Have often thought about the need to simplify still further our *Rule of Taizé*, beginning with the title. It is not at all a rule in the normal sense. It tries to point out a simple path for living a parable of communion.[10]

May 6, 1974

The woodpecker is silent. His favorite haunt, the dead catalpa tree, has been cut down and burned. Its ashes will be used for glazing in the pottery. A tree falls! I still remember the old chestnut tree which had to be cut down one day after lightning had split it in two. Here on our hill, the rock is close to the surface and the soil is not very good. So every tree counts.

May 7, 1974

Late last evening, four Africans arrived. Two of them are exiles from their homeland. I stirred up the fire in my room, made them welcome and listened to what they had to say. One told how his parents were killed, simply because they belonged to a certain ethnic group. In this corner of Burgundy, they now have a new family.

May 8, 1974

Letter from a young Portuguese poet: "On April 25th, the poorest people in Europe showed that it is possible to achieve a revolution without violence.[11] It is a date to remember. A flame of hope is burning in our land. You could say that a child has been born, without too much suffering. At the moment, we do not know what

---

10. Brother Roger continued to reflect on the meaning of a monastic rule. In 1980, he included *The Rule of Taizé* in a book entitled *The Sources of Taizé*. In 1990, he simplified it and entitled it *The Little Source of Taizé*. After Brother Roger's death, the old *Rule of Taizé* was republished alone in 2010, and then included in the first volume of his collected works in French. A French-English edition of that rule was published in 2012 by SPCK in London.

11. On April 25, 1974, Portugal experienced what came to be called the "carnation revolution," putting an end to over forty years of dictatorship by Salazar and then Caetano.

color its eyes will be, but its first cries were so wonderful that a whole people woke up with joy. Pray that this newborn hope will grow and flourish. I have been longing to send you a telegram with these simple words: come and see."

May 10, 1974

It would be easy to inform the press of the difficulties we encounter with certain men at the head of church institutions. We would win immediate sympathy but it would be too easy; we would be working against the communion of the Body of Christ. It is an exercise in self-restraint to remain silent at such times. Try to understand those who oppose and perhaps one day, unexpectedly, a person-to-person talk will take place and everything will suddenly become clear.[12]

May 11, 1974

All through Christian history, great renewals have happened at times when there was burning love for the Word of God.

That fire dies down as soon as the Scriptures are frozen into a system, hardening into doctrinaire attitudes as cold as ice. People today are so aware of this that there is a certain instinctive mistrust of all "*ex cathedra*" teaching, even when it is firmly rooted in Scripture. They prefer to prove God by living rather than by reasoning. In their eyes, practice comes before teaching. A young theologian told me the same thing in his own way: "orthopraxis comes before orthodoxy."

12. A discrete allusion to a difficult episode, known in the community as the "summons to the Holy Office." On April 29 and 30, Brother Roger was called to Rome with three of his brothers for a meeting at the seat of the former Holy Office, with the Congregation for the Doctrine of the Faith and the Secretariat for Christian Unity. He had to give explanations about the presence of Catholic brothers in the community and the welcome of young Catholics at Taizé. On May 4 Pope Paul VI, having heard of the incident, expressed to Brother Roger in a private audience the trust of the Catholic Church.

May 17, 1974

In the *Rule of Taizé*, obedience is never mentioned. When I was writing it almost twenty-five years ago, I was aware that great changes were taking place in human consciousness. Whatever their motivation, people today try to use to the full the unique gifts they have received. They see obedience as inhibiting.

Yet no community can long survive, steadily moving ahead over mountains and valleys, unless it accepts in its very center the pastoral service of one person, just as no cell in a human body can remain alive without a central nucleus. This person's principal service is to lead each to discover his own gift and freely contribute it to the common creation.

June 7, 1974

Increasingly convinced, in recent years, of the existence of a whole realm of darkness, imponderable but active. Is it not visible in encounters when a disguised need to dominate arises, or a slight breeze of inquisition begins to blow? The believer is the favorite victim, being more exposed and defenseless.

This conviction goes contrary to current popular opinion that the tempter does not really exist. That we have got rid of the devil with his cloven hoofs as one of the terrors of the past is just as well. But who could forget that Christ faced the tempter for forty days?[13]

June 12, 1974

Rest your heart in God, let yourself float on the safe waters, loving life as it comes, with all the rough weather it may bring. Give, without counting how many years are left, not worried about surviving as long as possible.

13. See Luke 4:1–13.

June 18, 1974

A few days away from home, and I miss it already. It was just the same when I was a child. The first days spent away from home were holidays with my father's mother. I used to set off with incomparable delight. Once there, I would spend hours listening to her. Dressed in black, erect and motionless, she used to talk about the tremendous grief of her childhood, how her mother had declined and died in the space of three weeks, made blind by constant weeping over the family's troubles.

After only a few days, I would be bored. I used to long for home, to see the familiar house and the trees. My aunt, who lived with my grandmother, must have played a major part in that boredom. She used to spend all her time re-educating me. "You don't put your fingers on the sharp edge of the knife. You keep your hands on the edge of the table, not too far forward. You don't put your hands on your knees." I felt that my aunt was criticizing my parents. She considered my father much too simple in his tastes, and felt that my mother attached more importance to music than to her nine children. Everyone dreaded that aunt's remarks, so it was always the youngest who was sent to spend holidays with her!

July 2, 1974

At the end of next month, the Council of Youth will open. With all the suggestions received, it had seemed certain that by now we would already have the light needed to live the opening. Not at all. This feeling of emptiness is unexpected, hardly foreseeable, but by no means a real trial. Our confidence is not shaken. On August 30, we shall set out on this new stage with the little we have understood, and nothing more. Then the void will be filled.

Why this confidence? Because the Council of Youth is so little our affair, and so much Christ's. We shall simply be eyewitnesses, astonished and sometimes amazed. All that is authentic and vast in our undertakings must come from him. There are voids that stimulate a greater certainty.

July 13, 1974

There are people who are dying of a thirst to dominate and who, to maintain their existence, attempt to annihilate others by word or look. When, in their confusion, they employ analytical notions only half understood, they are considered authorities; they learn how to act the great expert and wreak their havoc. Never harden yourself when faced by destructive individuals. But never join them in that prison of their own choosing.

July 20, 1974

Meeting with a group of young Asians, North Americans, Africans, Latin Americans, and Europeans to discuss the opening of the Council of Youth. They think that one expression of this opening will be a letter addressed to the People of God, to communicate the aspirations burning in the hearts of the young. They have begun to work on it. For my part I will try to write another letter, addressed to each young person, to point out a few essential lines of force around which a whole life can be fashioned. A kind of little "rule of life" to accompany people through the years. It could be called "A life we never dared hope for."

July 25, 1974

For years now we have been searching for reciprocity between the Northern and Southern hemispheres, and yet the gap shows no signs of being filled in. Everywhere, condemnations and intransigence. There as here, young people are generous in the extreme. But this generation is doubly victim: because of a divorce between separated Christians that has weighty consequences, and an economic system in which some are anesthetized by poverty, and others by the uncontrolled urge to consume.

August 30, 1974

The day has come, this opening day of the Council of Youth, the day when we all long to say: open yourself to understand each person fully, each woman and man, made of the same stuff as you and who, like you, searches, struggles, creates, prays. The day has come after great expectation, nourished by a common search, with all the tensions which that involves. And what has finally prevailed has been a love that trusts.

On August 20, 1940, when I arrived in this human wasteland, there was nothing to suggest these days when so many young people would be gathered together at Taizé. And all those far away as well, those very dear to us who are reduced to silence, imprisoned, mistreated because of the Gospel and their struggle for justice and freedom. With all of them, with people from every part of the world, we are being called to a life that exceeds all our hopes.

The following entries were published in 1979 in a volume entitled Étonnement d'un amour *(The Wonder of a Love).*

September 4, 1974

When I was young, at a time when Europe was torn apart by so many conflicts, I kept on asking myself: Why all these confrontations? Why do so many people, even Christians, condemn one another out of hand? And I wondered: Is there, on this earth, a way of reaching complete understanding of others?

Then came a day—I can still remember the date, and I could describe the place, the subdued light of a late summer evening, darkness settling over the countryside—a day when I made a decision. I said to myself: if that way does exist, begin with yourself and resolve to understand every person totally. That day, I was certain the resolution I had made was for life. It involved nothing less than to return again and again, my whole life long, to this irrevocable decision: seek to understand all rather than to be understood.

September 5, 1974

With the opening of the Council of Youth a week ago, we leapt over a wall. Beforehand it seemed so high. We could have fallen back on the same side. Yet here we are, over it. A leap like that was not without a few bruises. But on the very afternoon of the opening, after the meal, my usual nap was peaceful, in spite of the fact that many thousands of young people were on the hill, and with them many church leaders, for the most part overflowing with friendship, though some were reserved. Ahead lie other walls to leap over, other hills to climb. In the struggles to be waged, we will still manage to listen to the voices of children and the singing of birds, the ones brought by Paco from the Canary Islands for the opening day. . . .

September 7, 1974

We have received piles of messages and telegrams. Clement[14] has to answer them all. His is the merry laugh that so often lightens our fatigue; all at once he is slightly overwhelmed.

September 9, 1974

As a sign of the stage we have reached, we have asked the young people to give up the small groups and special cells started four years ago. Perhaps we have not emphasized enough that this was in order to create new signs: small provisional communities that spring up everywhere, communities that see themselves as part of the church, in solidarity with the People of God and with a local identity. It would be taking the easy way out to act in the name of the Council of Youth or of Taizé. That would mean unconsciously involving themselves in forming a movement or even, ultimately, one more church.

14. Brother Clement (Laurent Laufer, 1936–2004), from French-speaking Switzerland.

Several times in the past people have urged us to start a new church. Such an undertaking would have given the lie to our quest for reconciliation. It would have meant entering into an age-old process that has torn apart the Body of Christ in the past. We have suffered too much from that process to make use of it ourselves. Those who have set out to create a new church have often experienced extraordinary enthusiasm at the outset, but in time the usual failings cropped up once again.

September 10, 1974

Remarked last night to Hassan: your presence here guarantees that soon we shall be unable to speak of the love of God without discovering the treasures of trust in Him found in the tradition of your family of origin, Islam.[15]

September 14, 1974

Gripped by the arrival of a group of young Vietnamese. A girl told everybody in church: "It's the first time we've been in a country at peace where we can listen to the birds and talk freely, with no whistling of rockets, no bombings, no sleepless nights spent looking for shelter in the trenches."

September 18, 1974

Becoming aware of a secularized world makes us hesitant to express what could distinguish us, as Christians, from the rest of humankind. It is true that, in the heart of God, the Body of Christ is as vast as humanity, and the thought that even one human being could be left out seems incredible.

---

15. Although the great majority of the visitors to the hill were of Christian background, young people from other religious traditions also made their way to Taizé, sometimes even staying for a certain period of time as volunteers.

September 21, 1974

Days made memorable by departures for distant lands. In one week, the same words spoken three times to those who were leaving us: you are going to find tyranny, executions, killings. In the presence of Christ, weep over your nation; let us pray together for that beloved country.

October 2, 1974

Before he returned to Africa, a young man from Congo told us about the death of his friend Jonas. Last May, he had set out with others for a meeting in a village as part of the preparation of the Council of Youth. A boat had an accident and Jonas was drowned. Some felt he had been murdered for political reasons. His parents declared that "he died for God." This evening we celebrated a Eucharist in communion with Jonas. When he was alive we could say to him, "Pray for us." More than ever now it is possible to keep on saying the same words to him. . . .

October 8, 1974

The stakes of what we have begun must be high indeed to bring with them trials I cannot allow to show for fear of discouraging even the most stalwart.

October 11, 1974

Vienna. Invited by Cardinal Koenig[16] to the closing of the synod of the Austrian church. I found him the same man who used to come to eat with us in our apartment in Rome during the Vatican

---

16. Franz Cardinal Koenig (1905-2004) was archbishop of Vienna, Austria, from 1956 to 1985. He was deeply concerned with ecumenism, serving as president of the Vatican Secretariat for Non-Believers. In that capacity, he attended the opening of the Council of Youth at Taizé.

Council. In him we can sense what openness to everybody means; he is a man who shows what the church is going to become.

The prospect of speaking in his cathedral from a raised sanctuary, which makes one feel so isolated, aroused some apprehension. The fear vanished as soon as we entered that place of prayer together and paused before a glorious figure of motherhood—a centuries-old painting of the Virgin Mary hanging on a column.

October 12, 1974

Quite spontaneous meeting with some young Austrians. We were packed close together, too many for the confined space of a Baroque church in Vienna, yet we managed to communicate. They had drawn up a list of questions, all dealing with current concerns, some of them blunt, like this one: "How not to be repelled by church institutions?"

Yes, institutions can alienate us, brand us indelibly, sometimes cause deep humiliation. But we can also alienate ourselves, by fighting against them. Christ never calls us to crusade against anyone. He does not ask us to use our energies to abolish, but to fulfill.[17] He himself did not abolish the fossilized institutions he faced, those of the old Law; he strove to fulfill them.

Creating communion with Christians who wound us does not mean compromising, of course. Love is not blind.

October 13, 1974

Frankfurt. Speaking in public in Germany for the first time, I have a vivid memory of a young German prisoner who died close to Taizé during the winter of 1945–46.

In 1940, when I settled alone in Taizé, it was, of course, to prepare a place where a parable of communion could be lived. But it was also to give shelter then and there to political refugees, mainly Jews. I was in Switzerland helping someone to cross the

17. Cf. Matthew 5:17.

border when, in November 1942, the Gestapo broke into the house at Taizé and I was compelled to stay away for almost two years. In 1945 the situation was reversed and camps for German prisoners were set up in our locality. I was allowed to invite some of these prisoners to the house every Sunday morning, for a short time of prayer and to share with them the food that was so hard to come by. Poverty was our common lot. Among those who came Sunday after Sunday, a young Catholic priest stood out. His whole being shone with serenity.

It was a time when, more than ever, hatred engendered hatred. One day, some local women whose husbands had been deported to Germany and killed in concentration camps, in an act of strange desperation, attacked one of the prisoners. The one they fell upon was none other than that young German priest. In his weakened state, it meant death for him. During his last hours, there was nothing in his heart but peace and forgiveness. I saw what I had known for months: he was a reflection of God's holiness in the fullest sense of the word.

In Frankfurt, I told this story. And as modern technology made it possible for me to be heard simultaneously in both Germanies,[18] I told my listeners that any of them who had tragically lost a father, brother, or husband could contemplate him in the face of that young priest.

October 20, 1974

With the young brothers, the Eucharist is celebrated in the house, near the Coptic icon showing Christ with his hand on his friend's shoulder. We remain kneeling there for a long time.

---

18. Since the end of World War II in 1949, Germany was divided into two countries, the German Democratic Republic, linked to the Soviet Union, and the Federal Republic of Germany, linked to the West. The residents of East Germany could not travel to the West, but could listen to Western media. Following the construction of the Berlin Wall in 1961, Taizé brothers and young people sent by Taizé frequently made covert visits to East Germany to create links with Christians there who could not cross their borders.

Last Friday, after a similar celebration, we were asking one another how our vocations had come about. We all agreed that the origin of a vocation was surrounded by ambiguities. But some could see the starting-point in a kind of visitation, an annunciation, confirmed as time went on. The words "annunciation" or "visitation" came so spontaneously to their lips. Men of the previous generation would have repressed such words. At that age they would have been wary of putting into words the unique experience of one who aspires to follow Christ.

November 10, 1974

On this Sunday afternoon in Notre Dame cathedral in Paris, the wish was expressed that I should speak as I do every week in Taizé—saying a few words about the Gospel, giving news, and dealing with the most urgent questions in the hearts of the young. But here in this venerable cathedral, everything is different. When I was a boy we used to listen as a family, with our headphones on, to the Lenten talks broadcast from Notre Dame. Father Samson's voice was like the prophet reaching us high up in the Jura Mountains. I am astounded to find myself, a man with no talent for oratory, speaking in the same place.

In addition, there is no simultaneous translation. At Taizé, that makes it possible to be heard in several languages at once, which simplifies everything. I am in the habit of telling my brothers who are interpreting in their booths: translate just as you want to; say something else if you think it best; it doesn't matter in the least. Then everything is easier.

As we left, some people were distributing leaflets. When we come across this kind of extreme pronouncement, we should at least be glad that the authors have had this chance to vent their bitterness.

November 11, 1974

Yesterday in Notre Dame cathedral I quoted the African who, just before he left for home, was worried: "In the days just before the opening of the Council of Youth, I wondered whether people would understand the *First Letter to the People of God* we were working on, if people would grasp its strong language and its basic intention. The day it was read out I was relieved; the young people had realized that it was not mainly about ourselves but about the Body of Christ, the church, called to be a worldwide community of sharing. Our intention had got across; we were not making a destructive analysis, but expressing demands that can only be made of those we love."

There are some who find it hard to understand that we associated ourselves with the text of that letter to the People of God. In its sometimes vigorous language they did not recognize Taizé's usual way of speaking, as if we had somehow wandered off the beaten track.

It is true that tone often counts more than content, and that it would be possible to see that letter as a premature pronouncement from on high. Those who wrote it, however, wanted nothing other than to put into practice the song of the Virgin Mary, when she calls for greater unity among human beings and when she says that, by the coming of her Son, "the powerful will be cast down and the poor lifted up."[19] The letter draws directly upon that woman's words. Why does the intuition of the Virgin Mary, expressed in the language of today, upset certain older people?

That young African was right. The *Letter to the People of God* can only be understood in its context. It was written by young people who, for four and a half years now, have been constantly returning to the starting-point, the threefold celebration of the Risen Christ. Since Easter 1970 they have been meditating on these words: "We celebrate the Risen Christ in the Eucharist, . . . we celebrate him by our love for the church, . . . we celebrate him in our brothers and sisters. . . ."

19. Luke 1:52.

November 21, 1974

Letter from some political prisoners in Chile: "On the 30th of August, in prison, we celebrated a Mass to ask that the opening of the Council of Youth go well. We have just finished arranging a little chapel in the prison; it will be a place for worshiping Our Lord."

November 23, 1974

Many are finding it difficult to stand an autumn wetter than any in living memory. And yet it is possible these days to turn one's attention within. The oak log in the fireplace gives off little explosions. Under the eaves there is a pile of twigs for feeding the fire; their local name is *charbonnettes*. Without them the flames would die down; the log would smolder and give no heat.

The last ten years pass before my eyes, in particular the growing numbers of young people coming up to this place of prayer. When our Church of Reconciliation was built in 1962, its huge dimensions were hard to accept. And now it is often too small.

So many conversations suggest that the desertion of the churches by the young will continue to increase. Little communities spring up but seldom manage to last, to the point that the uncompromising words of Christ come to mind: "When the Son of Man comes, will there still be faith on earth?"[20] There is no answer except to continue with the young people, some of whom cover enormous distances, even in winter, to come here. At the moment there are some from Australia, Finland, and Norway.

November 27, 1974

Francisco has just lost his young wife. She was only twenty-five. There was a car crash involving all the family except himself. In the ambulance she was just able to say to him and to his son Martinho, "I love you." These Portuguese immigrants, who live in the

20. Luke 18:8.

village, are such close friends of ours.[21] We go to see him; I sit on his right, Daniel on his left. From time to time it is obvious that his heart is broken. He can only lay his head on my shoulder, sobbing helplessly. Several times he says, "Our God directs all things." He knows that his two children are out of danger. His is going to live for them. "I will be everything for them; I will always stay with them."

On Sunday morning, a few hours before the accident, Martinho happened to be beside me at the Eucharist, and together we went among the people bringing the peace of Christ. As always, he was dancing and hopping along, with the happiness of a child who is loved. He would learn of his mother's death on leaving the hospital. What a burden this child of six will have to bear now! Unlike an adult, he cannot see things in perspective. He will know in his own flesh the meaning of the words from the Second Vatican Council which have remained with me more than any other: "Man is sacred by the wounded innocence of his childhood."[22]

November 28, 1974

In general we bring our deepest humiliations on ourselves. Why wear ourselves out looking for their cause elsewhere?

21. In the wake of two families from the south of Spain welcomed by the community to live in the village at the end of the 1950s (see entry for September 28, 1972), Brother Roger invited two Portuguese families to come to Taizé. The one he speaks of here arrived in 1971. Other families would follow in succeeding years, from Vietnam, Bosnia-Herzegovina, Rwanda, and then, after Brother Roger's death, refugees from Iraq, Sudan, Afghanistan, and Syria.

22. Discourse by Pope Paul VI at the closing of the Second Vatican Council on December 7, 1965: "The church of the council has been concerned with man, . . . man sacred because of the innocence of his childhood, because of the mystery of his poverty, because of commiseration for his suffering."

November 30, 1974

Leaving for Rome, as every year at this time. Yesterday evening, conversation with Jean-Pierre.[23] He himself is surprised at what he said the other evening when we were all together. It was something he had never before put into words. That evening, he spoke of his happiness. And yet for years his work has been monotonous and exacting, answering the telephone while typing out letters and texts. All that labor is not child's play. I often hesitate to ask him to type revisions of the same text several times over. But Jean-Pierre assures me that for him, his work is part of a whole where everything has its place. The secret of his happiness? He does no more than hint of it: the certainty of a presence.

December 2, 1974

Fatigue surfaces as usual at the beginning of a stay in Rome, after a long period of work at Taizé. Joyful walk across the Piazza Venezia. Up to the Capitol for the panorama of the city. After Mass at the *Gesù*, we remained in the huge empty church, going from one spot to another. A crib has been put out for the Christmas season. Churches are lovely when they make you feel at home, and you can come and go as you please.

December 3, 1974

Welcomed Enzo and his wife.[24] Not so very long ago, his features showed the weariness of a boy who had to rise very early in the morning to help his parents clean offices. Today he is a young scientist engaged in nuclear research. With his team he has just succeeded in isolating a particle. He has been working intensely and his transparent face shows the effects of lack of sleep. His voice is

23. Brother Jean-Pierre (Bouvier, 1918–2013), from Geneva.

24. One of the sons of the concierge at the Via del Plebiscito in Rome, where the brothers rented an apartment during the years of the Second Vatican Council; it has continued to serve as their residence in that city.

hoarser than usual. Sofia and he talk about the young Christians of Italy. They see them exploding into many little groups and trends which cannot possibly come together. They are extremely worried.

December 8, 1974

Max went to the Piazza di Spagna for the prayer in the open which takes place every year on this day. The pope noticed him and told him he would like to see me.

Even if the weight of Roman institutions could be crushing to anyone who let himself succumb to discouragement, coming here every December is still essential. Peter died in Rome. Christ entrusted to him a definite charge in the church. It is for us, by our burning confidence in him, to help the bishop of Rome divest himself of enormous structures so that his ministry becomes more and more that of a universal pastor, exercising for all Christians an ecumenical pastoral vocation and leading the church to become a ferment of communion throughout humanity.

December 9, 1974

Why are Christian youth movements disappearing? Many young people like to meet together to reflect on the Gospel, to pray, and to look together for commitments in society. But organized movements hold little interest for them. What new means can we find with them of rooting their lives in Christ and in the essential of his message?

December 14, 1974

Return to Taizé. Once again the Bois Clair looms ahead, overhung by a long black cloud—a narrow corridor that has to be gone through in order to reach home. The choice of the village of Taizé remains a mystery. Why, at the beginning, did I not stop fifteen kilometers further on, among the open hills overlooking the plains of the Saone River?

December 22, 1974

A brother hands me a page of a letter to read over. It came several months ago from a Young Christian Worker:[25] "To link us with the ecumenicity in which I profoundly believe and which strikes me every time I come to Taizé, speak, Brother Roger, for the young workers. Many of them are looking to Taizé. I am going to bring some fellows from the factory to the opening of the Council of Youth; that will lift our action into the dimension of the universal. But speak, brother, speak for the others."

Speak! But what can one man's words do? All together, yes, we can speak. Four and a half years ago, when we announced the Council of Youth, it was already the same question: what can one man do alone? Not much. But together, with a clear vision of the People of God, we shall live a life we never dared hope for.

December 29, 1974

In the plane, with Robert, on the way to Latin America. Before the opening of the Council of Youth, powerful suggestions had been made. I had been asked to go to places where things are critical, alone or with young people, depending on the situation. The country where a visit seemed most necessary this year is Chile. To go there to listen, pray, and try to understand the poor and all who are giving their lives.[26]

In our luggage is the episcopal ring that belonged to Bishop Larrain. At the end of the first session of the Second Vatican

25. The JOC (*Jeunesse Ouvrière Chrétienne*) was one of the movements of French Catholic Action in the postwar years.

26. On September 11, 1973, a military coup d'état overturned the elected government of Salvador Allende and replaced it with a junta under the direction of General Augusto Pinochet, suppressing human rights and exercising a violent repression.

Council, when he was returning to his own country, that Chilean bishop slipped off his ring at the airport and said to a friend, "Take this to Roger, as a token of my faithfulness in the ecumenical vocation." Misunderstood throughout his lifetime, that man had to deal with the most incredible cross-currents imaginable as he worked to create a new awareness among Chilean Christians. He was also one of the founders of the Latin American Bishops' Conference. If he had not died in an accident, he is the one to whom we would be making our first visit. Since we never keep anything of value in our house, his ring will be passed on to his successor, the present bishop of Talca.

December 31, 1974

Short stop in Mexico for a gathering of young people from this country and all the countries of Central America, in a poor neighborhood of the city of Guadalajara. We did not come here in order to run a meeting; we are making a visit to discover in human faces reflections of the face of God.

1975

The situation in Chile continued to preoccupy Brother Roger, following the visit he made to that country in early 1975. Events in the rest of the world, notably Poland and Africa, were not forgotten for all that. And of course there was the life at Taizé, with meditations on nature, relationships among the brothers, and reflections on the inner life. The year's end found the prior of Taizé once again in Rome, at the Eucharist for the end of the Holy Year 1975, which was intended to be a year of reconciliation.

January 1, 1975

Today the Holy Year begins. The organizers in Rome wrote to ask me to send a message for the young. Before leaving for Latin America, I wrote them the following words:

"Originally a jubilee was the announcement of a year of celebration. Could this year of reconciliation be a celebration of forgiveness? You are members of the youngest generation of Christians: will you be able to help your elders make it a year of peace? In every reconciliation, in every communion restored, new vitality and a new springtime come into being. This springtime will mean the end of our mutual condemnations, the old ones and the new ones. And in our turn we will be bearers of friendship and reconciliation for those around us, creators of peace with all, even with those who do not share the faith of Christians."

January 2, 1975

Warm welcome at Santiago de Chile. The cardinal is at the airport.

A simple journey like ours answers people's longing to be visited in the dark periods of life.

January 3, 1975

This morning we were shown our program, planned out hour by hour. At the top of the list, a meeting with General Pinochet. With the situation as it is, seeing him is out of the question.[1]

Among the many meetings today, one conversation with a few young people will remain with me. The word church constantly recurred on their lips. They had had many reservations about it previously, but they now see the church of Chile becoming just

1. Brother Roger's refusal to greet General Pinochet had an immediate repercussion on the program for his visit: the authorization to visit political prisoners, at first granted, was then refused. Only during a subsequent trip to Chile five years later was Brother Roger able to take part in the Christmas Eve celebrations in a women's prison.

what they were hoping for—a place where everyone is listened to, a house where non-believers are brothers and sisters of believers. At the end of our meeting one of them, who knows what it means to commit one's life to the cause of justice and who has gone through agonizing ordeals, summed up what really mattered for them: "To live out a radical commitment to the Gospel in a situation which humanly speaking is hopeless, we are seeking to be the salt hidden in the earth."

January 4, 1975

The Committee for Peace plays a unique role in this country. It is made up of about a hundred people who give themselves unsparingly, visiting those in difficulty, helping prisoners and people under arrest, and feeding undernourished children. At its head, a young priest who has been to Taizé, Cristian Precht. He is constantly on the front lines.

January 5, 1975

Visit to a base community in a poor neighborhood. We pray with them. A young couple puts us up for the night in their shack. We all sleep in the same room, with the four children, our beds separated from theirs by a few pieces of wood. One of the children has an earache and cries all night long. Through the slits in the planks, cold blasts blow in from the Andes. The dogs howl for hours on end. A night of waiting. A vigil.

January 6, 1975

The most impressive meeting of this visit to Chile—with Madame Luis Corvalan. She is of Indian blood. At fifty she seems so very young. Her husband is in prison, her eldest son has been tortured.

Until we met today, Madame Corvalan had not understood how it came about that Pope Paul VI had intervened one night and prevented her husband's execution. She did not know that we telephoned from Taizé to Rome that night to ask the pope to intervene at once.

At the end of our conversation this woman, wife of a Communist leader, said, "Do tell people in your country that there are Christians here who are a light." She herself is probably not a believer. As she was leaving, she asked if she could come back in the evening with other wives of political leaders in the previous government. She also spoke of their tortured children.

"Salt of the earth," the young man said the other day. "Light for others," said Madame Corvalan today. The very same paradox as in the Gospel. Salt hidden alongside the oppressed, with no obvious effect, but at the same time the light of the world, bearers of an enlightening word or a liberating action.[2]

January 13, 1975

Back at Taizé. Martinho comes to see me regularly after school. He knocks at the glass-paneled door and comes in with quick, light steps. Two months ago, he would have told a story straight out of his imagination in a loud voice. Since his mother's death he enters without a word, silently gives me a hug, pulls up a stool and stays a moment or two leaning against me. If I am talking to someone he acts as if he doesn't see them, even if they know each other well. He, the fearless one, lowers his eyes as if staring into a void. The void is there: a mother, the most caring of mothers, has disappeared.

January 25, 1975

From Latin America, the Council of Youth seemed to me like a gentle breeze bearing along a few seeds of communion. A breeze carries, without being visible in itself.

---

2. See Matthew 5:13–14.

All communion is both strong and fragile at the same time. It is strong when, even without our realizing it, part of the robe of Christ, that robe which is the church, is being woven, with many and varied threads: some bright and joyful, others dark with human blood. But we also know that communion is something fragile—we here on the hill are people who have never wanted to create a movement or attract a following.

February 8, 1975

Letter from one of our brothers living in Bangladesh. The need there is considerable. He reports these words of a young Bangladeshi: "If you have come here to add one more project to all those that have already been brought from the West, go back home. But as you have come first and foremost to pray, go and get all your other brothers and bring them here too."

February 22, 1975

At our yearly council meeting, we looked for a sign to live out, one with no ulterior motives, that would point the way to love for the church. The only answer is the call to holiness. The distinctive feature of this call is a joy which does not come from us; an Other clothes us in it. Is it difficult to discern the presence of that Other? Sometimes we call him the Stranger. And yet he is there all the time, now in light now in shadow. It is we who are far away, we who are loath to live the combat of the light. This combat is real! That of watchers in the night. Will we be those watchers in the night of the church?

February 27, 1975

When I leap out of bed, a surprise: trees and fields bathed in midsummer light. Two sparrows have settled in the nesting-box nailed to a branch of the lime tree. They come and go, disappearing into the dark hole where their brood awaits them. At the window you only need to lift your eyes at any moment to notice birds, just now the blue-tit with its pale yellow breast.

February 28, 1975

Invited to speak in the cathedral of Saint Pierre, Geneva. How could I not think back to the time, more than thirty-two years ago, when we used to go every morning to pray in this very church with young people? After the first two years at Taizé, when we had to flee from the Gestapo, Geneva became our place of refuge.

March 6, 1975

For the first time Alain[3] tells me the words he has repeated to himself over and over again for many years: "Jesus my joy, my hope, my life."

March 17, 1975

Conversation with Angelina[4] on abandoning oneself in God. It is when we are being buffeted on all sides that we get up again most quickly: one blow counteracts the effects of the previous one, one difficulty drives out another. Leave till later the worries that assail you. It is true that what some people write about us cannot leave us indifferent. A visit from the writer of the most cutting remarks revealed all the makings of an inquisitor. He is one of those who batten on the spoils of others.

3. Brother Alain (Giscard, 1929–), a Frenchman who entered the community in 1949 after witnessing the life-commitment of his own brother Robert. He was active in setting up a cooperative farm, the COPEX, with other farm families close to Taizé.

4. Angelina Camps, from Barcelona, was active in the preparation of the Council of Youth and made many visits to young people in Europe and on other continents, particularly in Latin America. She later joined the Sisters of Saint Andrew.

March 20, 1975

Re-read the letter written to me, four months before he died, by a psychiatrist whose reputation had spread far beyond the borders of his own land.[5] He already knew how serious his illness was: "For some time now cancer has lost its hostile, alarming character. It has the role of a loyal collaborator, a kind of stimulus helping to change many things in me, stirring up, challenging, and opening up new and vast perspectives."

In that man prayer and action were one. In the short spiritual testament he left behind, he reflects on the possibility of turning human weaknesses to advantage. He admits that for a long time he suffered from a sense of his limitations. "Then came the time when I realized that the very acceptance of this feeling of insufficiency and limitation could bear fruit. I must not look at what others are doing or at their abilities, but rather recognize my limitations and fully accept them. That is the source of liberation and, as a result, I have no need to compare myself with others or look at their abilities. The feeling of inferiority and the impression of being excluded have contributed enormously to my growth as a human being. They have given me access to myself and this is so important for my patients: not only to be able to accept them with their fears and their weaknesses, that goes without saying, but still more, to know that those fears and weaknesses have their positive side, that they can lead to something good."

March 29, 1975

The eve of Easter. After two months of an early spring (never in living memory has anything like it been seen), icy cold grips us. The young people who have come for Holy Week are floundering in mud. At night, in the church, some fall asleep on their knees, in prayer.

In Dahomey, a young African priest, Alphonse Quenum, and six other persons were recently condemned to death on political

5. Dr. Peter Rutishauser, from Zurich. See *Brother Roger's Journals*, 1:114.

grounds. Sent today this telegram to the president of the Republic of Dahomey: "With thousands of young people gathered at Taizé we learn of the seven death sentences, including that of Father Quenum. In the name of human dignity pardon them. Do not wound the conscience of the young."[6]

March 30, 1975

Easter morning. Meditation on the Bible text "Be faithful until death and I will give you the crown of life."[7] Perseverance is not a law. It is a continual creation. It is also the struggle to live a love with no turning back, a communion with the Risen Christ one's whole life long. Loving to the very end does not come naturally; there are dead-ends, crises, failures. And the inner tug-of-war starts up. He is at it, the tempter; he tempted Christ, and to us he whispers, "Stop persevering." And at times he insinuates, "You know, other loves will refresh your loving." Go right through dead-ends and failures, don't avoid them or bypass them; pass from one stage to another stage. Whoever perseveres in giving their entire life gradually discovers, at every turn, another life welling up: the life of the Risen Christ.

6. Until November 30, 1975, Dahomey was the name of the country now called Benin. Under the Marxist-Leninist regime of President Kerekou, Father Alphonse Quenum was condemned to death for his struggle for freedom and truth. He was imprisoned for ten years and pardoned in 1984. A historian and theologian, he would later become rector of the Catholic University of West Africa. He died in 2014.

7. Revelation 2:10.

April 9, 1975

Letter from our brothers Michel[8] and Bruno.[9] Enough to keep me singing all day. Bruno tells of the Brazilian slum where he works. "I could not keep going were it not for your letters. . . ." And Michel: "In Paraguay among the poor peasants, I spent an austere Holy Week. Perhaps it was not so bad, it gave me the chance to come to terms with the difficulty I had in leaving Taizé once again. Five weeks in the community, surrounded by the warmth of our brothers, was enough to make Latin America seem very empty at first. But I am discovering too that our life with a few brothers in Brazil is authentic enough to keep on stimulating us."

April 12, 1975

In the spiritual wasteland of present-day Europe, how can we point to the only way out of the darkness and the fog? For at least a century now, the old world of Europe has been slowly sinking into an ocean of skepticism or indifference; what parable can we offer to lead people to draw their life from God? A few years ago, Europe seemed to be in a pre-revolutionary state. Today that revolution bears the names pessimism, despair, nihilism, and introspection.

April 18, 1975

Yesterday evening, took a walk in the meadow, westwards. Gusts of cold wind blew from the north. The clear sky promised a night of frost. Near their shed the newborn lambs were beginning their dance which, every evening for two months, they have been doing

8. Brother Michel (Bergmann, 1936–2009), born of German missionary parents in New Guinea, went to secondary school in Australia and then studied sociology in France and Germany. He spent most of his life in Brazil as the brother responsible for the *fraternité* there. He died on a visit to Australia as a result of a freak accident while swimming in the ocean.

9. Brother Bruno (Toedtli, 1940–), Swiss German, later ordained a Catholic priest in Brazil by the local bishop to help with the pastoral ministry of the poor diocese.

at the same place. In the distance, a small grey patch on the grass. Walking along the hedge, I found a little lamb lying on its side. I carried it away, its head resting on my arm. It had the look of the newly born. When I took it to the shed it seemed too weak to be interested in the milk bottle. Then, as it gradually warmed up, it began to suck. This morning I hurried to visit it: had it survived the night? It was there, wiggling its tail at the sound of my voice.

April 19, 1975

Conversation with Eric's father.[10] In spite of his seventy-eight years, this pastor cannot give up the ministry. He fills in for others. But as he frequently has to change parishes, he is sorry that he can no longer keep a steady contact with those he meets. Retiring seems to him to be the antithesis of the Gospel. He questions the bureaucratic procedure by which, in Christian circles, someone's destiny depends upon the laws of efficiency. In reality, it is towards the end of life that the insights gained by long experience are harvested. If the ministry is interrupted, the mainspring runs down. We remain alert and energetic when we know that our life will continue to be of value to God and to others until our dying breath.

April 22, 1975

The little lamb is dead. The peasant in me is deeply affected.

April 23, 1975

Mealtime conversation with Oscar. This young man from Burundi has just learned of his father's death. He does not know the

10. Jean de Saussure (1899–1977) was an influential preacher and theologian in Geneva, named pastor of the cathedral of Saint-Pierre in 1929. He was very supportive of the brothers during the community's early years. His son Eric (1925–2007) joined the community in 1950 after his studies in the fine arts and was known for his artwork as a brother—paintings, etchings, stained-glass windows, and icons.

circumstances.[11] This morning he came running up to talk about it, his face lined with grief. After the Eucharist celebrated in memory of his father, we attempted to exchange a few words. What could we say? Oscar is the head of the family, and his exile prevents him from joining his relatives. Listening to him brings to life the nightmare a large part of Africa is going through. He is cut off from his country, for how long he has no idea. To console him by speaking of the day when he will see his family again would be to plunge him into illusion. Are we going to be passive spectators of the tragedy of so many nations? At the very thought, a gaping void opens before us.

April 26, 1975

A mild night. In the distance, through the white mist lit by the full moon, the outlines of the hills of Cormatin and Bray are visible. Happiness: there it is, within reach. Never seek it; it would only flee. It lies in attentiveness and in wonder. Happiness seems sometimes to disappear for a long, long time. And yet there it is, when eyes meet. There it is, close at hand, when a man loves without really knowing if that love is returned. And if, as well, that man feels loved by many others, then he ought to be filled with a happiness beyond words. . . .

April 29, 1975

The parents of Alois[12] tell how, after the war, they had to leave the village in Eastern Europe where their families had lived for two

11. The political tensions in Burundi over the years led to massacres that in 1972 caused many victims.

12. Brother Alois (Löser, 1954–), born in Stuttgart, Germany, was chosen by Brother Roger to be his successor as prior of the community, a ministry which he exercised from 2005 to 2023. His parents, of peasant stock, came from the German-speaking region of what is today the Czech Republic; they were expelled after the Second World War along with all the others of German origin.

centuries. The parents of both of them did not survive being uprooted from country life. And their own roots, too, are still in the village where they were born. What kept them going? The father replies without a moment's hesitation: prayer. And Alois adds: it was a repetitive prayer, the rosary.

April 30, 1975

End of a thirty-year war in Indochina. How can I not hear once again the voice of the Vietnamese man from Hue who was here shortly before he died in the bombings, and who prayed in our church: "Lord, I am afraid of my fear"?[13]

May 5, 1975

Letter to a great-niece: "You know, you are dearly loved by your family, your Uncle Roger included. You are loved, you and each member of your family, by God, and by Jesus Christ, for ever. Now that you receive him in the Eucharist, you can be sure that he is offering you a fount of living water. You will understand this little by little. But as for the Eucharist, you will always receive it with the heart of a child, whatever your age."

May 10, 1975

Enchanting, all that the eyes take in. The coolness of the brief showers. Sunshine again, and each blade of grass has come alive. The happiness of the springtimes of childhood. Setbacks and shadows are washed by the light rain, swept away by the warm light of a copper sunbeam. And the race begins once again, leaps for joy alternating with expectations disappointed. In these little things a zest for life is engraved like filigree, a source without which everything would be insipid.

13. See *Brother Roger's Journals*, 1:84.

May 12, 1975

For my sixtieth birthday, my sister Genevieve[14] prepared a meal with all her household. The food was simple, but we stayed at table for a long time. Is it still possible to laugh so much at our age? Aunt Mathilde, at ninety-four, too deaf to hear everything, laughed to see us laughing.

May 14, 1975

Gregoire and Johan set off to spend four months in Finland. Even in the far north of the country, young people are waiting for them. This arouses in them a little apprehension. So we tell each other: instead of being too worried, suppose we look on the coming months as poems of communion?

May 18, 1975

Cristian Precht has arrived, the Chilean priest who organizes all the efforts for mutual aid among the poor after the coup d'état. In the midst of serious tensions he has to solve thorny problems.

Together we discussed in what ways we could be in solidarity. At this very moment winter is setting in in Chile, with rain, dampness, and cold. We cannot remain indifferent to a kind of genocide of women and children which comes with the winter months.

May 25, 1975

On Piekary Hill, near Krakow, pilgrimage of a hundred and eighty thousand men who work in the mines of Upper Silesia. They arrived this morning, long processions of them. First they received

14. Genevieve Schutz (1912–2007), Brother Roger's youngest sister, joined him in Taizé during World War II to help with the welcome of refugees. After the war, she acted as a mother for twenty war-orphans raised by the community. She never married, and lived in Taizé for the rest of her life, having given up a promising career as a concert pianist.

communion during the night in their various parishes, then they set out in buses and trains, finishing their journey on foot. Invited to speak to them on prayer just after Cardinal Wojtyla's[15] sermon, among other things I entrusted this intention to them: so many priests in Western Europe are isolated, whereas in Poland priests are supported by a whole nation of believers.

The Polish people has a unique vocation. In the course of a thousand years of history, it has amassed a treasure of generosity and perseverance. The constancy of its faith sustains the hope of many Christians across the world.

May 28, 1975

Letter to Aniela Urbanowicz:[16] "I am reliving the time spent in your home in Warsaw. In my mind's eye I can see the many tokens of your hospitality, the wild flowers and garden flowers in the shallow bowl on the table. I wish you could have seen the vast forest, so close to Russia, where we went at the end of our stay to take home an old peasant who had come by train to Warsaw for the sole purpose of meeting us. Would it be possible for the young man who drove us there to take you to see those landscapes and those skies, some of the most remarkable in Europe? I am going to sit down and write about those landscapes, and I think that many people will go to Poland to see them, to listen to the silence of those woods where the singing of the birds takes on a surprising resonance."

This aged woman, who lost her husband and her daughter in the concentration camps, brings out the true selves of many people, young and not-so-young. Her trust awakens intuitions in them. Her welcome in Warsaw was exceptional.

15. The future Pope John Paul II.

16. Aniela Urbanowicz (1899–1988), an active member of the Polish intelligentsia, visited Taizé in 1960 and became a lifelong friend of the community. She translated the *Rule of Taizé* into Polish and was instrumental in making the community better known in Polish Catholic circles.

June 2, 1975

Walk with Marc on the path by the oak of Mamre. A slight breeze from the east has been blowing since daybreak: like the wind in a ship's sail, it lends a lightness to everything, even to speech. Marc is talking about a young man from an Eastern European country. We have no news of him and his luminous face comes to mind, as if wafted by the breeze. And once again, the eternal question: "Why him?"

June 10, 1975

In a dream I sail along the coast of Chile, with its pitiful hovels made of mere branches. Since coming back from Latin America, its people are with me even deep in the night. If the resistance of the Polish people is exemplary, that is because they fought against invaders for centuries, a selection was made, characters were formed. But what is to become of the Chilean people, who have never in their history been forged in the fires of such trials?

June 12, 1975

Received these surprising lines from Pedro:[17] "Today an old Portuguese woman reported to me what she had heard in the course of an ecumenical meeting from the lips of the president of a Protestant church: 'At Taizé there are crucified men who have seen the truth but do not proclaim it, so as not to break the unity of the church.' I just had to send you these words."

July 12, 1975

Why are we here on the hill, we brothers and the young who come week after week?

17. Brother Pedro (Foz Coma, 1947–), from Barcelona. Spent several years living with a small group of brothers in Hell's Kitchen, New York City.

We are here to be taken hold of by God, worked upon by him and inwardly changed. This transformation cannot come about overnight. Continually we have to be transformed all over again. It is far from monotonous, this search for God!

What is the goal of this transformation? To become capable of accepting wholeheartedly events easy to deal with as well as hard times and oppositions, always ready to go towards what lies ahead.

If we do not allow ourselves to be taken hold of, we should not be surprised if we understand nothing about God and consider him a mere object of curiosity or interminable discussions; our life turns round and round in a never-ending monologue with ourselves. We may be able to understand many aspects of life and of the world by ourselves, but it is not so with knowledge of God. We know God only when we allow ourselves to be taken hold of and worked on by him from within.

July 25, 1975

Letter to one of our brothers who is living among the poorest of the poor and whose courage is boundless: "My dearly beloved brother, I keep reading and re-reading your last letter. Your lines transmit, with uncommon force, a breath of life. Our little community, loved by God and even indulged by him in so many regards, is able, through some of its brothers, to go to the extremes of loving and to suffer with the outcasts of society. All your powers are called for and laid bare in the service of the poorest, to such an extent that even your health is affected."

August 4, 1975

Went to Macon with Patrick.[18] Heavy traffic made us take the old road, the one we used to take in the early years, on our bicycles or even on horseback. Everything invites us to go frolicking, the little

18. Brother Patrick (Robert Stahl, 1926–), a French brother who often served as Brother Roger's driver.

valleys running around the vineyards of the Maconnais, the forest stretching as far as the valley of the Saone River, the narrow road, squeezed in between hedges, woods, then fields and houses with their long galleries. But, spurred on by work, we are torn from our unfinished dreams and the car seems to sprout wings and fly. On our return, Taizé comes into view clinging to its hill, supported on its rocky foundations, against a dazzling sky, incandescent with the sun's heat. The constant need to admire is satisfied.

August 6, 1975

Today, as we celebrate the Transfiguration of Christ, we sing at the same time the unimaginable prospect of our own transfiguration. Christ enters us, and changes us into his likeness. He transfigures everything in us, the good as well as the bad.

In every man and woman there is a wound, inflicted by failures, humiliations, and the guilty conscience prompted by moral injunctions and psychological explanations of every sort. This wound may have been caused at a time when we needed infinite understanding, and nobody was there to give it.

Moan about this wound and it becomes a torment, an aggressive force against ourselves and against others, generally against those who are closest to us.

Transfigured by Christ, it is changed into a locus of energy, a source of creativity giving rise to a potential for communion, friendship, and understanding.

August 7, 1975

Thought again intensely about those women we met in Poland, peasants who told of their six years of deportation along with their children in the camps of Siberia. To one of them, a humble peasant woman, I said, "You lived the martyrdom of Jesus Christ." In simplicity of heart she answered with one word: "Yes." That visit to a Polish village is the kind of event someone experiences only once in a lifetime. If there is any harmony still to be found on this earth, we owe it to those who have made the hidden offering of their lives, for the church and for humanity.

August 14, 1975

Murder of my soul,
buried in dark desert nights,
my being, silence,
come back Jesus.

Letting the pen run on produces these strange accents. Latent puritanism constantly desires to kill life; it is ashamed of spontaneity; it wants to murder the soul, disguising as positive injunctions what is only destructive violence.

August 17, 1975

Many older people have been invited by the young to spend a day at Taizé. It is so true that Christian communion is like an invitation to a meal prepared for all, without exception.[19]

Now, everywhere in the world, we are discovering people who have been forgotten, who are missing from the feast. They are sometimes in places where we least expected it. Some can be found in old churches, women and men who are waiting for Christ but who remain alone. Among them are many shepherds of the flock,

19. This was called "a day of the People of God." As the *Letter from Taizé* explained: "The Council of Youth is not outside of the church. It is not a new movement; it is not a reality reserved to the young. It is a common commitment to seek a new face of the church, a joy lived together within the People of God, a joy that is centered on the risen Christ. . . . Young people will go in pairs to visit parishes and Christian communities in different countries to look together for ways of understanding the Easter mystery: Who is Christ, the Risen Lord? From what wellspring of love and life can we draw to become women and men of communion?" Cardinals Marty and Doepfner, respectively presidents of the French and German bishops' conferences, as well as Philip Potter, secretary general of the World Council of Churches, were present that day at Taizé.

priests or ministers who suffer intensely from isolation, who are so forsaken that they even wonder what good their ministry is.

This festival of communion would not be complete if we did not find some way of including those who, though nonbelievers, are our brothers and sisters. It is up to us to welcome them without ever making any of them feel that they are being trapped.

September 19, 1975

Tirelessly Christ seeks us and is at work in us. He keeps on asking: Do you love me? Do you love me more than anyone else?

That is because our relationship with him is one of friendship. And just as friendship knows periods of indifference, in our life there are times of indifference to Christ. And then we wonder: Have we left him?

No friendship can grow without new beginnings, reconciliations. When we are reconciled with Christ, we discover him as if for the first time: the love of all loves, maltreated, wounded, rejected by many and yet never tired of accompanying us.

September 20, 1975

One day Saint Teresa of Avila and Saint John of the Cross met for a meal. Grapes were brought in. "I'm not going to eat any," said John of the Cross. "Too many people have none." Teresa answered, "I, on the contrary, am going to eat them, to praise God for these grapes." Their conversation mirrors one of the tensions of the contemporary church.

September 21, 1975

Discover fragments of humanity in the most dehumanized individuals, flashes of generosity in the most hostile.

September 22, 1975

Talked with a couple. They are in great difficulty with two of their children. What can be done to help them through their troubles? How to convince them that if their children have grown apart from them and even from God, they need not worry about their future? They have already given the best of themselves by a kind of osmosis, and this best will emerge when the children take on responsibilities in life, perhaps when they in turn educate their own children. Then they will have to sift all they have assimilated and it is the very best, the pure wheat handed down from their parents, that they will retain.

September 23, 1975

Be attentive to God's silence. It is often more tangible than his signs.

September 24, 1975

Long conversations with Martin.[20] His mission among the poorest is going to take him far. He will be so alone, in the center of Africa. In spite of the value of a departure like this, the heart's reasons count for more and make every long absence of a brother hard to bear. Only the trusting of faith allows us to consent to such missions.

October 11, 1975

It can happen that someone discovers violence against father or mother in their heart. Generally speaking, this feeling is not exteriorized in words, and that is just as well. Urges which can be quite

---

20. Brother Martin (Hoffman 1937–). A Swiss German who spent many of his years in the community as a brother on other continents, notably Africa and North America.

drastic dwell within all human beings. If people expressed all their latent aggressiveness to one another, it would be disastrous. Violence and jealousy are in the human heart. Stirring up these murky waters in the name of sincerity and truth leads only to loss of vitality and energy. That should be kept for our dialogue with someone who has received the ministry of declaring God's forgiveness.

October 12, 1975

Communion in the church is sometimes threatened by those who wield ecclesial authority in order to assert themselves, in extreme cases to compensate for some frustration.

But there are also shepherds who have persevered in a whole lifetime of faithfulness. Sometimes their ministry has only been exercised for a small number, recognized only by a few. Aware of the feeble resonance of their priesthood, they arouse our admiration. What words can be found to tell them to what degree they are the salt of the earth? Often these words stick in our throat, and perhaps it is better that way: the value of the gift of their lives is indescribable.

October 23, 1975

What do you wish for your brothers? Freedom. Not an autonomy that would make individualists of them, but the freedom of communion, the freedom that does not infringe upon the liberty of another.

October 24, 1975

A flowering of mystical vocations would raise the hopes of a church in mourning.

November 9, 1975

Two children, in dark clothes, arrive timidly at the church. Six and eight years old. Their names, Marie and Henri. We open a picture-book at the page where there are two children and I tell them: here are Marie and Henri and, close beside them, Jesus. Then we discuss who to pray for. The next day, Marie talks to her parents and insists that the family stay till the evening prayer. As that is impossible, she comes out with: "It wasn't worth it being here just for one day; better not to have come at all." After that, how can we fail to let the prayer of children show us grownups the way, we who are so ready to believe that prayer must pass through the intelligence, be explicit and logical?

November 14, 1975

Came across this Chinese proverb: "If you want to work for a year, sow wheat; for ten years, plant a tree; for thirty years, train others."

November 15, 1975

Maria de Lourdes Pintasilgo, Portugal's representative at UNESCO, is spending a few days at Taizé.[21] We are still hoping for a springtime of Lisbon. Such a springtime is essential if the younger generations in Europe are to keep alive their hope in humanity. They are tired of so many political experiments that, one after another, have come to nothing.

November 16, 1975

The Chilean government has just dissolved the "Committee for Peace." Immediately sent this message to Cardinal Silva, the

---

21. Maria de Lourdes Pintasilgo (1930–2004) was prime minister of Portugal from 1979 to 1980, and later member of the European Parliament from 1987 to 1989.

archbishop of Santiago: "After my journey to Chile, I kept quiet. Today, after the dissolution of the Committee for Peace by the Chilean government, I cannot keep silent. In Santiago I saw with my own eyes the work done with unflagging courage by this committee, to give aid to the most destitute and hope to those in despair, especially children. I have confidence in your powers of discernment to find ways of continuing this work. With so many others in Chile you are a living witness to the Risen Christ, in agony until the end of the world. Rest assured of my faithful support."

November 20, 1975

In the years before I turned twenty, I was plagued by the fear of lacking intellectual honesty. I refused to affirm a faith I could only dimly sense. But I was searching. And one day I came across this verse of a psalm: "My heart says of you: seek his face. I am seeking your face, O God."[22] All at once I realized that I could kneel down by my bed and say that very prayer: everything within me says, seek his face: I am seeking your face.

November 28, 1975

A few moments spent with Denis.[23] His room has lost the look of an architect's office; the weaving-loom has replaced the machine for copying blueprints. This brother, who took first place in the College of Architecture's final examinations, is unemployed. The office where he worked has no orders now. Intelligence is engraved on his features. He is still young, but like so many others these days, he has been forced for the time being to stop using skills that took so long to acquire.

22. Psalm 27:8.

23. Brother Denis (Jean-Daniel Aubert, 1934–2015), originally from French-speaking Switzerland. An architect by training, he designed the Church of Reconciliation. He later spent many years in Africa as the brother in charge of the fraternités in Nairobi (Kenya) and Senegal.

December 6, 1975

Impossible to leave for Rome this year without thinking of the words spoken by our brother Christophe eighteen months ago at an ecumenical meeting in Geneva, a few hours before the stroke which was to cause his death: "The year 1975 will be both the year of the General Assembly of the World Council of Churches and the Holy Year, which Pope Paul VI would like to make a year of reconciliation. May reconciliation remain at the heart of our searching." Those were the last words of that contemplative.

December 17, 1975

Finished the letter to the pope, which I will put into the hands of Paul VI tomorrow:

"In order to find a way out of one of the dead-ends of ecumenism, for years now we have seen the necessity, in spite of centuries of separation, of living in a communion of love and trust with the pope, the bishop of Rome.

"Concerning the ministry of the bishop of Rome I have been led, in the course of these years, to sum up as follows the hopes and expectations of many:

"First of all, people want the universal pastor to be concerned with justice in the world and in the church. It is up to him, therefore, to show not only the Catholic church but the non-Catholic churches as well the way towards great simplicity of means and the refusal to rely on economic or political powers in their ongoing journey.

"Second, people also want the bishop of Rome to do all he can to enable the reconciliation of Christians to occur, without asking non-Catholics to repudiate their families of origin. Even with a view to a communion that is more universal, more ecumenical, truly catholic, repudiating is contrary to love. Even in the interests of a greater love, people cannot, in conscience, wound their love for those who brought them to birth in the faith. Among those who handed down the faith to them, there is very often a father and a mother. Could the bishop of Rome, then, open the Eucharist to any baptized Christian who believes in the real presence of the Body and Blood of Christ, and who passionately seeks the unity of the faith, without requiring any repudiation from them? (Today I would write: without asking them to be a symbol of repudiation.)[24]

"Now at the end of this year of reconciliation, I have come to Rome with one specific intention. In the search for reconciliation among Christians and with all people, it is imperative to find simple but concrete acts to accompany words of reconciliation.

"For years now you, as universal pastor, have asked for forgiveness, if any blame could be attributed to you for the separation of baptized Christians.

"For this reason we at Taizé, together with many others, earnestly desire one thing: to ask forgiveness of the universal pastor, the bishop of Rome, for age-old or recent divisions among Christians, as well as for the delays in the search for reconciliation.

"Ours is a poor voice with little authority. It is by no means adequate to reply to your words. And yet, to keep silent in this year of reconciliation would seem to me a betrayal of the Gospel.

"Is it not essential to devote all our energies to continuing the Holy Year by concrete acts of ecumenical reconciliation, acts that the Holy Spirit will indicate in response to our ardent searching?"

December 18, 1975

Audience with Paul VI. As I usually do in these intense conversations with the pope, I brace myself against his desk. Like any good man from the countryside, once the body is firmly in place, the dialogue can get going. Following the method Paul VI likes, I have prepared a report which he has already read, and on which we will base our conversation.

At the end of every audience, the pope indicates that the meeting is over by taking in his hands the gift he has prepared. This year it is a photocopy of a ninth-century missal. Then the

24. This phrase was added by Brother Roger when preparing these journal passages for publication in 1979.

pope, who is not a spontaneous man by nature, concludes for the first time by saying, "I am going to embrace you."

December 24, 1975

Invited to stay on in Rome for the Christmas midnight Mass, celebrated by the pope to mark the end of the Holy Year. This unexpected extension affords the chance to welcome some people from Lebanon. We search together with them: since words can do nothing to extinguish the waves of passionate hatred that are breaking over their country, could there be another way? How to love those minorities that feel threatened? And how to love those majorities who imagine that the solution lies in their superior strength? How to understand the person who has lost all sense of direction and who explodes into the violence of words, and sometimes of arms?

1976

In 1976, as the Council of Youth continued to stimulate reflections and gatherings in Europe and on other continents, Brother Roger made an important decision: to go to Calcutta and Bangladesh at the end of the year with an intercontinental team of young adults. Their intention was to live among the poorest and write a Second Letter to the People of God, *which would urge Christians and others to live out a "parable of sharing" in a world where the gap between rich and poor was widening disastrously. Unexpectedly, as a result of his collaboration with Mother Teresa and the Missionaries of Charity, Brother Roger brought back with him to Europe a baby from Calcutta, Marie-Sonaly, who was raised in Taizé and for whom he took on the role of a godfather.*

January 3, 1976

Commit everything to you with the heart of a child. Abandon myself to you with or without words. Entrust to you all that goes against my heart or upsets my plans; pray for my opponent. Ask, even when I no longer dare to, as if every request were marked with the seal of self-interest. Ask anyway; take the plunge, knowing that you answer according to your designs and never ours. And sometimes even go so far as to cry out in pain, when trials abound and I cannot bear them all at the same time. Dare to use blunt, strong language: you understand it, even if others cannot. Entrust to you now and always whatever disturbs and torments me. And also keep silence in your presence.

Then, little by little, the praise of your love becomes the only thing that matters. Play within me, organs and zithers. Flutes, sing in me. A sound all at once both muted and jubilant: let nothing stop the indispensable praise of your love.

January 9, 1976

It is rare to find people who do not worry about the poor quality of their praying. In vain Christ assures us that we do not add one second to our lives by worrying[1]—we torment ourselves for not knowing how to pray.

January 10, 1976

For two days now, my sister Marie-Louise has been hovering between life and death. The victim of a car accident on her way to Taizé, her body is broken everywhere; she has eleven fractures. The breath of God unites in one and the same rhythm her breathing, as she suffers in her hospital room, and mine as I go about my daily tasks.

---

1. Matthew 6:27.

January 20, 1976

Muslims and Christians, brothers of ours, are killing one another in Lebanon.[2] A month ago a twenty-two year old Lebanese man, going back to his village to spend Christmas there, was killed on the road in an ambush. The young martyr had a presentiment that he was going to die. In his room at college he had left a letter to his family: "I have just one request: forgive with all your hearts those who killed me. Join me in praying that my blood, even though I am a sinner, may help to atone for the sin of Lebanon. Mingled with the blood of all who have fallen, from all sides and from all the religious confessions, may it be offered as the price of the peace, the love and the concord which have disappeared from this country and even from the whole world. Don't be afraid. What grieves me is that you will be sad. Pray, pray and love your enemies."

January 29, 1976

Annual council meeting of the community. We remind ourselves that we walk along a narrow ridge. Our vocation sets us on a knife-edge path. Day after day we face alternatives that bear the names mediocrity or holiness, stagnation or Gospel freshness, personal security or leaving all for Christ's sake.

The call to be a parable of communion is a road to holiness for us; it leads us to follow Christ in loving to the very end. And we know that love culminates in the ability to forgive. If the community is not a community of forgiveness, it becomes a countersign.

But the community is never there for itself. It exists to radiate Christ and the unity of his Body, the church. It recapitulates the church, a tiny image in the church in a perpetual state of creation. How can we take part in this creation? By what sign?

We make our way along a ridge, at the risk of feeling the attraction of the void and losing our balance. Keeping on through thick and thin, without slipping down on one side or the other. Although it may mean getting bruised, sometimes even being torn

2. A civil war began in Lebanon in April 1975 and would last until 1990.

apart; that is perhaps part of our vocation to holiness, a holiness that can only be lived all together. Our vocation is to hold firm at the intersection of currents and conflicts, in that unique communion called the church.

February 2, 1976

Conclusion of the council. To live out a vocation to universality, to remain present in different places across the world, to take new risks and even go to be with those who are in countries undergoing oppression, yes to live out a vocation to ecumenicity, the community needs as never before in its sails the wind of the open sea, the very breath of God's joy.

It is time, it is time, Lord, to let ourselves be borne forward by the breath of your joy.

February 24, 1976

Heart of my shattered heart,
who will soothe the secret lament?
Who will pour oil on the biting pang
that never dies?
Christ, do you hear the words held back?
You are there, a love most soothing.

When all within is serene, why these lines? I am certain that the years to come will be for singing God's praises.

March 21, 1976

Writing many letters means living so intensely with each correspondent that it would scarcely be a surprise, on raising my head, to meet his or her eyes above the page. The pen runs on, swiftly, and as it runs the heart causes it to discover what the mind had no inkling of a moment earlier. No point in re-reading letters, if words or ideas miss the mark never mind, re-reading would take away the spontaneity of the first flow and steal precious time from the writing of more letters.

March 25, 1976

A young Protestant asks me how to face the dryness, sometimes the emptiness, of his prayer. When, in his heart of hearts, someone knows that they are loved for ever and ever, they are not afraid to wait in silence, even if some silences were to last until death.

April 1, 1976

After attending the adoration of the Blessed Sacrament at Notre Dame cathedral in Paris, a brother remarked: on such occasions you rediscover the great Catholic tradition of France, and you go away the greater for it.

April 4, 1976

A few days ago Fabienne came in with a sweater that her aunt, my sister Genevieve, had just washed. I offer her some dates and ask her what is happening at school, if she likes playing the harpsichord (she is very gifted), and, now that she is ten, if being the eldest of five brothers and sisters is not too much responsibility for her. To all these questions she replies only by nodding slightly and muttering "Hmm, hmm." Why is she so shy? Was she scared by a dog on her way here? Her big laughing eyes give no clue. The following day her parents tell me she didn't know what to do with the date-stones, so she kept them all in her mouth until she couldn't speak a word.

April 5, 1976

Meeting of young people in Brussels Cathedral. In these last few days, all the good reasons for escaping the ordeal of leaving Taizé to speak in public kept piling up—it is so much better to listen to individuals in personal conversations; it is so difficult to leave the many young people already here twelve days before Easter. It was a good idea, though, to agree to take part in this congress of the World Federation of Catholic Youth Movements, because we do so want the Council of Youth, far from serving itself, to have the vocation of offering a service to the church, to tendencies which already exist or which are coming into being, to movements, to young people, priests, nuns, and brothers.

April 9, 1976

Surprising conversation with some university students from Iran, who had come to spend a week at Taizé. They are Muslims, but they speak the same language as so many young Christians do: they do not go to the mosques, for they consider practicing Muslims to be mere conformists. They are looking for ways of arranging little corners for prayer in the mosques when they return home.

April 14, 1976

This morning the hill is resting under a great woolly sky, a vast fleecy rug with patches of vivid blue. In the woods the charred undergrowth has given place to a riot of gold against brilliant green: a kind of ranunculus with jagged petals has spread into the farthest corners. But this enchantment is short-lived.

April 15, 1976

Many discussions with young people in preparation for Easter. In the course of the winter, there has been enthusiastic searching after new ideas for the next stage on our way forward. Some have been responsible for reading and listening to the many suggestions that came in from everywhere. Some days their heads were full to bursting.

We are aware of the enormous tensions that are shaking our societies. In the midst of a situation where sclerosis is setting in, it is important to open up ways towards a hope rooted in Christ, the hope of believers, and towards a human hope, one we share with nonbelievers.

How can we fill up the chasms dug by big vested interests, the powers of this world, who assert themselves by restricting or suppressing human freedom, and to this end use every means, including political imprisonment and physical and moral torture?

To counteract the effect of injustice and hatred, those inexorable driving-forces of history, we do not have the powerful weapons of war at our disposal, but only the violence of peacemakers, the violence of those on fire who take possession of the realities of the Kingdom of God.[3]

To live out all that lies before us, we will continue using poor means, a minimum of organization, and no bureaucracy; we will continue to refuse donations. It is so true that the moment you yield an inch in this regard, you wake up one fine morning compromised, at the mercy of financial interests.

April 17, 1976

Easter Eve. What sign can we announce to all the young people who have come from many different countries to say that there is only one human community, and that the rifts growing deeper between North and South are tearing the human family apart?

Next October, we will go with an intercontinental group of young people to share the life of the poorest of the poor, in Calcutta and then in Bangladesh. It is only a limited gesture, a poor parable, but it shows the direction in which we are heading.

In order to find ways of being a ferment of communion in a human community that is under increasing tension, it seems that the time has come to compose another letter to the People of God. We will write it in Asia.

---

3. Matthew 11:12.

April 23, 1976

In sending me the following lines, one of my brothers thinks that his experience may illuminate others as well as himself: "Two weeks after my return from Finland, as I was going into church one day, I suddenly saw God standing at the top of the sanctuary steps. His arms were outstretched in a gesture of welcome and he radiated boundless love, a boundless longing to welcome each person, the ordinary as well as the holy. If it has taken me such a long time to write this down, it is because I needed time to assimilate an experience both strong and fleeting, and to realize that perhaps it did not happen for my benefit alone."

May 16, 1976

Turin. Coming here to speak at a gathering of young people also means seeing Cardinal Pellegrino again.[4] In the midst of conflicts, he stands firm with infinite courage, at the cost, among other things, of being rejected by the powerful of this world. The ministry of this man, a son of the poor, is essential for the people of Piedmont. He has the insights so often granted to the very old. When I think of him I see him as a direct descendant of the church fathers. From the days of his consecration as a bishop, at which I was present, I realized that in him the church had a man of the sources of the faith.

May 31, 1976

Rudolf[5] passes by my window. A pile of letters in his arms—the mail from Germany. Just one day's letters, and each one has to be

---

4. Michele Cardinal Pellegrino (1903–1986), a respected theologian who served as archbishop of Turin from 1965 to 1977 and worked hard to implement the reforms of the Second Vatican Council in that city.

5. Brother Rudolf (Stökl, 1936–), German, one of the first brothers to travel and organize visits of young people in the countries of Eastern Europe during the Communist era. Later on he spent time in different *fraternités*, notably in Brazil.

answered. It is not for nothing that some brothers work late into the night, although in the morning the bells call all of us to prayer without exception.

June 4, 1976

A few moments in the pottery. On a blackboard where the young brothers who work there are in the habit of writing a quotation, there are these words: "Your love, O Christ, has wounded my soul; I go forward singing your praises." Are they the authors of such a profound thought? No, it was written in the seventh century by John Climacus in his old age. At the age of fifteen, he had entered the monastery of Sinai. He realized that a passion for Christ is expressed through a person's whole being, flesh and spirit.

June 6, 1976

Eve of Pentecost. Late this evening in the church, a luminous face, features of extreme pallor with silvery hair coiled round her head. At the age of seventy-five, a woman says words that sum up the intention of multitudes of mothers and grandmothers: "I have come here to pray for those who are losing the faith, for my grandchildren."

July 4, 1976

Reading a lot about the USSR and the United States. Two fascinating countries. Russia, with her people able to survive the most severe trials, rooted and bound to their land, in love with nature as few others. The Americans: after uninterrupted successes, feverishly pursued, now tormented by an anxiety they have never before experienced. On this day when Americans celebrate the anniversary of their independence, it would be enthralling to be there, to understand more. Next on the list, books about contemporary India. Underlying this constantly renewed interest in economics, sociology, and the social sciences is one recurring question: Where is God, where is Christ, where is the Gospel in all these nations?

July 5, 1976

Corrected the proofs of *A Life We Never Dared Hope For*. Selecting pages of a journal for publication is not a very appealing task. Some of the brothers chose the pages of the manuscript to be kept, the ones that comment, in detail or in general, on our ongoing life, shot through by a hope against all hope. Like *Festival*, this new book affords glimpses of a struggle to keep despair from getting the upper hand.

July 14, 1976

Three o'clock in the morning. Short walk in the meadow. Several times the cock gives his call. The crow wakes up and clumsily flies from his perch down towards the woods. The silence, broken for a moment by his hoarse croaking, closes in again. In the east, red light begins to play on the crests of the Tournus hills.

August 3, 1976

At this time of year when so many young people are at Taizé, all my inner resources are mobilized by the same question as thirty-six years ago. At that time, when I was called to lead a group of Christian students, the question was already the same: How to let people catch a glimpse of Christ, the poor man of Nazareth, visible beneath the surface in the heart of every person?

Now, in high summer, the main thing is to find words, week after week, to keep on telling people who this poor man of Nazareth is—the man who walks along our ways of darkness and illuminates them, whenever we let him look through our eyes. How often would it be tempting to give up this weekly meeting with all the people on the hill.[6] How is it possible to talk about him every week with fresh words? Will those who listen understand that he is alive, that he lives within them? Will they realize that he is knocking at their door?

August 5, 1976

As I write, a tiny beetle manages to climb upon my motionless left hand. He crawls along my arm, his dark stiff back gleaming with rich colors.

My joy in creation is ever present. As the days go by, it becomes indistinguishable from that other joy, communion with people. But, without a Presence more certain than all earthly realities, none of this happiness would remain.

Amidst the pressures of work and of meetings, sometimes when tempers flare, when urgent matters continually interrupt the work at hand, He is there, the One who sets us free.

August 17, 1976

Yesterday, visit from Mother Teresa of Calcutta. Together we composed a prayer: "O God, the Father of all people, you ask us all to bring love where the poor are humiliated, joy where the church is downcast, and reconciliation where people are divided—fathers and sons, mothers and daughters, husbands and wives, believers and those who cannot believe, Christians and their unloved fellow Christians. You open this way for us, so that the broken Body of Jesus Christ, your church, may be a leaven of communion for the poor of the earth and in the whole human family."

---

6. One evening a week, after the prayer in the Church of Reconciliation, Brother Roger spoke to all those present on the hill of Taizé. A system of simultaneous translations made it possible for all to follow his talk. It was the only meeting with everybody during the week; at other times the young people met in smaller groups.

September 10, 1976

Fields and woods hold festival; the light dances between fleecy dawns and sunsets, growing softer with every day. The festival goes on, with no end in sight. Yesterday someone said there had been too much rain last month, and yet only two or three heavy showers come to mind. At the end of the meadow, under the almond tree, there is hardly enough shade to sit in the morning. Down below, the vineyard, growing vigorously in its third year, is already laden with purplish grapes, promising well for its first wine.

October 19, 1976

In the life of the church the shepherd, the one who is at the heart of the living cell which a community is, has only one charge, to be a servant of communion. He is there to try to keep alive what otherwise would dislocate and scatter, to the point where one day the community would no longer be one.

On this eve of the departure for Calcutta, I reminded my brothers that, from the very beginning, I have never wanted to be called "prior" within the community. I am their brother. And in the last few years we have seen to it that outside the community, too, the name "prior" is only used in certain situations, to identify rapidly a particular charge.

For the same reason, years ago, I refused the Legion of Honor. Why? Because today it is impossible for those holding positions of responsibility in the church to add honorific titles to their service of God. They can no longer permit honors to be attached to pastoral office.

October 24, 1976

In the plane, bound for India. The meetings these last two evenings in the Stiftskirche of Tübingen, that church that is so symbolic of German Protestantism, and in the splendid Catholic cathedral of Münster, fill the heart to overflowing. The churches full of young people, the journey through Germany so far beyond anything we could have imagined: only the angels could find words for it. The friendship and the mutual trust between us and so many young Germans is a real force.

Through my words, even poorer than on other occasions, did they understand that anyone, of whatever age, who is willing to take risks for Christ and for the Gospel, is led, sometimes in spite of themselves, to share in the most unexpected adventures?

October 31, 1976

Fraternal welcome at Calcutta airport. In Indian fashion, young people had prepared the garlands of flowers that they always hang around the neck of a new arrival.

We had decided to come and live in a district of Calcutta so that the *Letter to the People of God* would be written among those who are familiar with the most widespread condition on earth: poverty.

The young people who went ahead of us, arriving from America, Africa, Europe, and from other Asian countries, already have a foothold. But they have had trouble finding a place to stay: families live in such crowded conditions and the large boarding schools are not suitable for us. It was only yesterday that we were told: there is a Catholic family, living in a very poor Muslim district, who will understand what you want.

And so here we are in the midst of this noisy neighborhood, full of children. Tonight we met the Joseph family. Living in three tiny rooms, they offered at first to accept only my four brothers and myself. Then they agreed that all the boys could stay here, sleeping on the floor. Finally, the mother said the girls could sleep upstairs with her. They have eight children. They are beaming. We realize right away that, beginning tomorrow, the eldest son could join our intercontinental team. They have already understood everything.

November 1, 1976

Early in the morning, everyone leaves for work. I myself go to the home for children found in the street. One little girl of four months, with a solemn face, attracts my attention. She lost her mother at birth. Sister Fabienne, who directs the home, says that this little girl ought to be taken to Europe, urgently. She is very delicate, winter will be coming soon and she will certainly be among the 50 percent of the children who do not have the strength to survive the bad season with its epidemics. And she adds: take her, save her, you can see that she is already attached to you, yours is the first man's voice she has heard.

November 2, 1976

Work at the home for the dying. An old man, about to die, cannot manage to swallow. He asks us to pray for him. A young man, lying further along, calls out. He makes a gesture with both hands indicating God, Allah, a look of profound intensity on his face. He lays his cheeks on my hands several times. He has great difficulty breathing.

In the afternoon, our first meeting together to prepare the *Letter to the People of God*. We listen to those who have already gathered intuitions from everywhere, whether at Taizé or in the course of journeys through all the continents.

November 3, 1976

A little walk in the alleys. Mohammed Yacine comes up to us and asks why we are here. He talks about the neighborhood: 25 percent of the people are unemployed, and half of those who work have no steady employment. He offers us tea. Mohammed Ismael, the schoolteacher, turns up. At first he speaks aggressively, affirming that all we are saying is in the Qur'an too; he tells us that Muslims never abandon one of their own in need. The conversation continues. At the end of our meeting, he apologizes for having been hard on us; he thought we had come with political intentions. He invites us to come to his school for a meeting with the men.

November 4, 1976

Starting today, an old Christian woman from the neighborhood is joining in our life and our reflection. She understands everything.

November 5, 1976

The temperature continues to be above normal, and the humidity at its peak. We all stand it wonderfully well, sustained as we are by the enthusiasm of our searching. The nights are short, the street noises intense. Transistors blare out Indian songs. All this noise goes on late into the night and starts again at five in the morning, when people begin to wash outside in the street by dousing themselves with water. The sewer flows past our courtyard gate; we have to cross it every time we go out and it has just begun to get even wider.

In two or three days, a simplification of our lifestyle has taken place. The people of the neighborhood are surprised that foreigners are willing to sleep on the floor.

November 6, 1976

Mother Teresa has sent us a little wooden tabernacle which we will use for the reserved Sacrament.

Visit to Pilkana, one of the largest slums of the city, seventy thousand inhabitants in an area seven hundred meters square. Human beings plunged into an ocean of tribulations.

Pilkana is that child, suffocating with tuberculosis, a Muslim. His mother says that now he does nothing but pray. Pilkana is the unforgettable beauty of the face of a young Christian woman with advanced tuberculosis of the bones who keeps repeating: today is a beautiful day. Pilkana is that old woman, dying on her doorstep, covered with putrefying sores.

Is it a collective sin that creates the existence of these Golgothas in a city replete with wealth?

November 8, 1976

From now on the young people of the team are working in small groups, in order to tackle a new topic every day—housing, prayer, work, possessions, the human family.

November 10, 1976

Received in Calcutta a letter from Latin America. A young man, the father of a family, announces that he has been set free from his political imprisonment. He, his wife and his two children will now go to live for a while with our brothers in Brazil:[7]

"It was your brothers and all who live lives of prayer that I remembered most during all my time in prison. In my solitude I was deeply conscious of God's presence. Now we are very happy to be given hospitality by your brothers; we feel at home with them. I lived for fifty days blindfolded, my hands tied, spending some days with nothing or almost nothing to eat, unable to communicate with anyone. They released me on condition that I leave my country, but they did not say for how long. Keep on praying for us, and for all the prisoners. Many of my companions used to say to me, 'I am not a believer, but pray for me.' I understand the contemplative life more and more. God knows what he is doing and it will all bear fruit."

November 11, 1976

Visit to the leprosy hospital with Mother Teresa. On the way she explains why, in the very first days of our visit and without asking

---

7. This young man from Argentina and his wife had spent a year as volunteers at Taizé a while back.

my advice, she had her sisters make me a second white robe. She doesn't understand why I don't wear it all day long. It's no good explaining that in Europe it is hard to wear a prayer garment outside in the street. She insists: you should never take it off, people today need this sign. To which I reply: I could not make that kind of decision without consulting my brothers.

In the leprosy hospital, the welcome from the hundreds of patients was striking in its spontaneity. They are all contagious. Many asked for the laying on of hands.

November 13, 1976

Leave for Bangladesh to visit our brothers there. While the group of young people remain in Calcutta, I take away with me the ideas already sketched out for the *Letter to the People of God* to consult the young people of Bangladesh.

November 14, 1976

To have brothers in Bangladesh, sharing the existence of people in a subhuman situation, is like seeing the flesh of our flesh become part of the poorest of peoples. The landscape is vividly beautiful, but housing conditions are beyond words.

Some forty young people have come from several parts of the country to meet us. With them we have long conversations and we take away with us Ranjan's question: "What way can we find to form one great human family?"

This country has behind it thirty years of troubles, from the bombings at the end of the Second World War to the catastrophic floods, not to forget the tragedies of the War of Independence.

November 16, 1976

Long conversations with my brothers on the meaning of their presence here.

Why do small groups of brothers immerse themselves in slums in Asia, Africa, and Latin America, to live there for years, when we know that these districts are more and more closed to Westerners? And why, with an intercontinental group of young people, did we enter a similar neighborhood in Calcutta?

Our presence is never in order to revive the process which involves coming from the Northern hemisphere and bringing our own imported solutions, no matter how valuable they may be. We know all too well how wary the inhabitants of the Southern hemisphere are of any relationship of dependency. If we go to these places, we do so in order to live a presence with no ulterior motives.

To the question "Do we go with absolutely no intention of accomplishing anything?" we would answer "No." Though we do not seek short-term effectiveness by bringing money or solutions worked out in the West, we do want to support local young people who are taking initiatives inspired not by us but by their own culture and their own genius, arising from the very depths of their own peoples. Such young men and women exist. They have concrete suggestions to offer. Like young Europeans, they are sometimes discouraged in the face of impossibilities, and in danger of falling into a skepticism that will lead them either to passivity or to violence.

We go to live with them in slums above all to live a parable of communion, always with only a minimum of material resources. And this in the company of the reserved Sacrament, which turns a rundown shack into a place inhabited by a Presence. Immersing ourselves in slums means living in the same way as the inhabitants do, and waiting with them for an event from God for their peoples.

November 17, 1976

At nightfall, a Sufi came in for a few moments. He wanted to speak a final word before we left Bangladesh. "All people have the same Master. Now this is still a secret, as yet unrevealed. But later on it will be discovered." And he went off again into the night.

November 20, 1976

Calcutta. A morning's work among children. Spent a long time with the premature babies. One of them, weighing almost nothing, his face lined with deep wrinkles, wanted to cry but had no voice. His mouth opened and he wept noiselessly. To be with these dying babies, holding them close, feeling their impotence as they suffer their agony, is like having one's heart torn out. Some cannot even feel the loving presence beside them and yet they suffer.

November 21, 1976

Inwardly preoccupied about the *Letter to the People of God*. To begin with, we were in a thick fog. After some time our eyes began to see. How could we remain blind when every morning we were doing the kind of work we had to do? Our hearts beat very strongly, but we remained dumb. Then our lips began to speak, And now it is the hand, still unable to write. The fog has not completely lifted yet. Late this evening the solution came to us. We are going to give up entirely the attempt to write a text containing too many abstract ideas, keeping only the concrete proposals.

There are many children around. They have a sense of rhythm; they sing and they dance.

November 22, 1976

At the home for the dying, the young man I saw the other evening seems to be better. He is like a skeleton, but perhaps he can be saved.

Here, what can we give except first and foremost human love? Going from one to another, stopping to spend a few moments with each one, telling them they are our brothers, our friends, or, the youngest, our sons. With them, the language of gesture is what counts. This morning a blind man kept placing my hands over his eyes. In laying our hands on them and praying with them, we have to remember their origins—Hindu, Muslim, or Christian.

It is true that in Europe we have our homes for the dying too. The only difference is that they are not obvious. When at Taizé I listen to many young people individually, I come across this one or that one, the son or daughter of divorced parents, who in addition may be suffering from a broken heart: they are like the living dead. In the home for the dying, as I pass from one to another, I find myself at times in the same situation as at Taizé, when in the evening some of the young people wait their turn to come and say a few words to unburden themselves of their despair.

And not only the young, but also middle-aged and elderly people who in their lives have loved much and now find themselves overcome by loneliness, their lives devoid of meaning.

In the present crisis of confidence in our world, how many are crushed by the mistrust of others, at those times when they are forced to recognize that their sincerest intentions have been distorted?

In our well-organized Europe, we too have our homes for the dying, but they are invisible.

November 25, 1976

Mass celebrated by Cardinal Picachy, the archbishop of Calcutta. It takes only a few Bengali lamps to transform our courtyard into a palace from the Arabian Nights. People are everywhere, even on the roofs.

November 28, 1976

Yesterday, owing to the censorship imposed in India due to the state of emergency, we could not send the *Letter to the People of God* by telex, so that it could be translated before our return for the gathering of young people at Notre Dame cathedral in Paris. That gave us extra time. We made the most of it and added a few introductory paragraphs: we had not yet found the words to explain why the essence of this letter was the parable of sharing. Today it has been done.

December 31, 1976

Since we came back from Calcutta, the little Indian girl we brought with us has been living in my room. At five and a half months, Marie-Sonaly is so delicate. She can only go to sleep in my arms. Day and night, it is amazing how she reacts to my voice.

Perhaps she has only a few more weeks to live. If she were to sense the growing worry I feel for her life. . . . Then I say to myself: if she dies, then you will talk it out, you will even argue, alone with God. But for now, entrust her to God. Resting on your heart, she will at least have experienced that trust God has placed in each one of us, and which is communicated through another human being. Let anguish be transfigured into confidence.[8]

---

8. Marie-Sonaly, the infant that Brother Roger met in the home for children in Calcutta (see entry for November 1, 1976) and brought back with him to Taizé at the request of Mother Teresa, did not die. Today she lives in France with her husband and young daughter.

Who Can Condemn Us?[1]

"Who can condemn us, since Jesus is praying for us?" (cf. Romans 8:31–36). As I listen to young people speaking personally to me, I often wonder what can be the source of the feeling they have of being condemned, that burden of guilt which has nothing to do with sin.

Sin is a break with Jesus Christ. It means using others, making them victims of oneself.

Now all human tendencies, the best and the worst, are summed up in each individual, but that is not sin. Yes, every tendency without exception coexists, to a greater or lesser extent: aspirations to generosity or to murder, the desire to kill father or mother, brother or friend; all the affective tendencies, love and hatred, all in a single being.

When some young people discover what they are and have no one to talk to, they conclude that they are little monsters, and they are driven to self-destruction, in extreme cases to suicide.

Who will condemn us? The norms of our societies? In every age, societies have spawned a process of self-defense, using guilt to force everyone into a mold with precise norms, a pattern of normality.

Before Christ, for example, little Israel, under constant threats to its existence, was anxious to ensure its continuity. So the barren

---

1. This was Brother Roger's Easter meditation for 1973, inspired by the question of a young girl (see entry for March 4, 1973). It was a topic that remained close to his heart.

woman was rejected and despised because, since she did not bear children, she had no place in the pattern of normality.

But for the Gospel there is no "normal" or "abnormal"; there are simply human beings, made in the image of God. The Gospel knows only one norm, the one who is supremely human, Christ.

If, in spite of our inner contradictions, we set out again every morning towards Christ, it is not with any kind of normality in mind. It is with the ultimate goal in view, the goal beyond our hopes, of being conformed to the very likeness of Jesus himself.

Who could condemn, since Christ is risen? He condemns no one; he never punishes.

Who could condemn? He is praying in us, offering us the liberation of forgiveness. We in our turn become liberators, not condemning anybody. Even in the struggle for human liberation, we are not going to be left in the rear guard. Perhaps every Christian is called to live as certain freedom-fighters have done, not hesitating to spend the whole night kneeling in silence before the reserved Sacrament?

Who could condemn? Even if our own heart condemns us, God is greater than our heart (1 John 3:20).

SELECT BIBLIOGRAPHY

Writings by Brother Roger

Brother Roger of Taizé: Essential Writings. Edited by Fidanzio, Marcello. Maryknoll, NY: Orbis, 2006.
Anthology with biographical introduction.

Dynamic of the Provisional. London: Mowbray, 1981.

Glimmers of Happiness. Chicago: GIA, 2007.
Brother Roger reflects on events and people that influenced his life and calling.

God Is Love Alone. Chicago: GIA, 2003.
The essentials of Brother Roger's thinking and personal accounts from the story of Taizé.

Peace of Heart in All Things. Chicago: GIA, 2004.
A brief meditation for each day of the year.

The Rule of Taizé. London: SPCK, 2013.
The original text expressing the fundamentals of the life of the Taizé Community.

Books about Taizé

Clément, Olivier. *Taizé: A Meaning to Life.* Chicago: GIA, 1997.

Santos, Jason Brian. *A Community Called Taizé: A Story of Prayer, Worship and Reconciliation.* Downers Grove, IL: InterVarsity, 2008.

Spink, Kathryn. *A Universal Heart: The Life and Vision of Brother Roger of Taizé.* Chicago: GIA, 1986, 2005.

DVDs (available at www.giamusic.com)

Moments in the Life of Brother Roger
Meeting Brother Roger of Taiźe

www.taize.fr

Information in twenty-eight languages about the community, meetings at Taizé and elsewhere (online registration), suggestions for prayer, the songs of Taizé, etc.

SUBJECT INDEX

Milton Keynes UK
Ingram Content Group UK Ltd.
UKHW010342140724
445551UK00003BB/23

9 798385 210596